War and Cleats

I THINK THAT SHE
STARTED "RESEACHING"
MORE THAN 30+ YEARS
AFTER I STARTED COACHING

AND A.Y.S.O. STARTED A
COUPLE OF YEARS BEFORE
THAT.

Dedicated to Marilyn and Victor Smith who always taught me the value of women's voices, particularly my own

Maya Bhave, PhD

WAR AND CLEATS

WOMEN
IN SOCCER IN THE
UNITED STATES

Meyer & Meyer Sport

British Library Cataloguing in Publication Data
A catalogue record for this book is available from the British Library

War and Cleats
Maidenhead: Meyer & Meyer Sport (UK) Ltd., 2019
ISBN: 978-1-78255-172-0

© 2019 by Meyer & Meyer Sport (UK) Ltd.
Aachen, Auckland, Beirut, Cairo, Cape Town, Dubai, Hägendorf, Hong Kong, Indianapolis, Manila, New Delhi, Singapore, Sydney, Tehran, Vienna

Member of the World Sports Publishers' Association (WSPA)

CREDITS
Interior & cover design: Annika Naas
Layout: Amnet
Cover photo: © AdobeStock
Managing editor: Elizabeth Evans
Copyeditor: Anne Rumery

Printed by C-M Books, Ann Arbor, MI, USA
ISBN: 978-1-78255-172-0
Email: info@m-m-sports.com
www.thesportspublisher.com

Contents

Acknowledgments

Any author recognizes that writing and completing a book may seem like a solitary journey at times, yet it never really is. The four-year research and writing path that led to this book at times certainly felt rocky and steep at times, but thankfully I was never completely alone in this process. First and foremost, I would like to thank my wonderful editor, Liz Evans, as well as Manuel Morschel and the entire staff at Meyer and Meyer Sport. They were truly a pleasure to work with. In addition, throughout the last four years I always had the support and encouragement of many people within the local Northern New England soccer community. There are so many people who encouraged my work, but a few were especially important. Special thanks to Jim Goudie, Dr. Roger Knakal, Kathie Desautels, Tess Swett, Shawntel Burke, Ben Hardy and David Saward for supporting, and in some cases giving input on, my work. In addition, John Mhyre, and the Vermont Community Foundation were pivotal in helping fund my early soccer research on middle and high school players. I also want to thank my colleagues at Saint Michael's College from the Sociology Department: Dr. Vince Bolduc, Dr. Robert Brenneman, and Dr. Amy Redman. Thanks also to Laura Crain, Lauren Stone, Liz Smith, and Rachel Lyons in the Saint Michael's College library, and finally a special thanks to my remarkable student assistants Jacquelyn Duffy and Cecelia Mullin. An additional individual who has been a steadfast, hidden component of this work is Valerie, my transcriptionist. Thank you, Valerie, for your numerous years of help. I also want to give a shout out to Joanna May Weinstein for doing some wonderfully swift, yet careful, editing, and Natalie Meyer for help on several charts and tables. Moreover, I am eternally grateful to everyone I met within the broader US soccer community, but particularly I want to thank the players and coaches I met throughout this multi-year project. I am honored and humbled that you took so much time to share your amazing stories with me. Thank you…

There are two dear friends, however, that were critical to the completion of this book. The idea for this book came from Dr. Kristin Novotny, and as my sister-friend there is no one else who knows so much about every detail in this book from beginning to end. It was her encouragement to extend my passion about middle school and high school girls' soccer into a larger manuscript that led me to taking on the wider research project. She encouraged me in this journey on my darkest days, celebrated with me during the best days, and always gave me incredibly sound academic advice and editing suggestions. Kristin, thank you for your abiding friendship, deep oceans of coffee breaks, and long hours of wonderful, insightful feedback.

Additionally, this book would not exist if James Franklin had not asked, "Will you come alongside and help us figure out why girls are leaving soccer?" I cannot say enough about all the things that James has taught me about soccer and youth sports in general. His steadfast belief that girls' experiences truly matter in soccer (and all sports) is refreshing and much needed in this often male-dominated soccer world where female voices often become obscured or are ignored. He truly believed in every part of my work and these detailed narratives of middle and high school girls are here because he bolstered the early process of this research. Thank you, James.

Finally, I have to thank my family. Thank you to my dearest mom who always encouraged and cheered me on through every single step of this process and continues to support my life and academic choices with incredible optimism. However, I would never have wandered near any soccer fields if not for my oldest son, Kieran. He has loved soccer since he saw and kicked his first soccer ball as a toddler, and he hasn't stopped kicking them since. I cherish the years we traveled with him to tournaments all over the US and beyond. Despite the fact that he will attest that sadly I *still* am not clear on many offside rulings, he knows that I relish every opportunity I still get to watch him play. This book would not have been started without Kieran's role in loving this beautiful game.

I also could not have accomplished this writing journey without the quiet, affirming support of my younger son, Eric. As a contrast, he plays competitive tennis, and many times his athletic journey inspired me through this process, not only because of his deep passion and enthusiasm for the sport, but because he is always the player to never, ever give up, at any point, in any match. Because he is my only kid at home now, he heard every detail of this book and saw all of my emotional ups and downs.

He, unfortunately though, bore the brunt of my stressful days and late night writing sessions. He never complained, and for that I am deeply thankful. As their mom, watching both of my sons play their respective sports continues to bring me an immense amount of joy.

And finally, to my husband, Anant, I could not have done this without your incredible, unwavering love, support, and keen insight as to when I needed to be dragged from my desk for red wine or whisky on the back deck. Thank you for telling me I could do this and for being as excited as I was upon completion.

Chapter 1

It's Just a Girls' Game:
Women, Sports, and Identity

Drive through towns as distinct as Waterbury, Vermont; Carol Stream, Illinois; Cary, North Carolina; and Modesto, California on a Saturday morning and you notice a common thread: hundreds of youngsters playing soccer at the town greens and recreation facilities. In fact, in the last forty years youth soccer participation in the U.S. grew 300% (Scavuzzo, 2015). Thus, we see gaggles of kids running up and down soccer pitches, bodies swaying while balls topple to and fro and eager parents perched on colorful folding chairs dotting the sidelines, actively waiting for their child to take their first touch. In many ways, sports and communities have been tightly linked within the American fabric in the 20th century (Nathan, 2013). Yet, if you look a bit closer, stop for a little while longer, there is something different about the scene now in 2019: the dominant sea of pink cleats, purple shin guards, matching scrunchies, and T-shirts that say "Yeah, I kick like a girl, try to keep up." Today, nearly half of the three million soccer players in America are girls, and in fact "there are now nearly three times more female soccer players in the United States than there are Girl Scouts" (Haner, p.175).

Yet what do we really know about these kids playing on these rec fields, in town parks and local elementary, middle, and high school facilities? Barrie Thorne, in 1993, wrote the definitive early gender piece on active children, aptly titled *Gender Play*. Her pivotal work on children, sport, and activity explored what gender meant on playgrounds (and in classroom settings) for female and male children. On the one hand she notes that gender to some is "an expression of natural difference" (p. 2), but she argues that in fact the feminist movement showed us that gender is actually "a social construction" (p. 2), something built out of our interactions and relationships. Thus, gender identity becomes more complicated than just simplistic notions of "boys will be boys," or "girls will be girls" (p. 1). Gender construction for Thorne (and modern feminists) is about female and male activity that is active, ongoing, multilayered, and dynamic (p. 3). I rely upon Thorne's analysis of gender, coupled with that of West and Zimmerman (2009) who argue that gender "is not a set of traits, nor a variable, nor a role, but the product of social doings of some sort" (p. 129) to explore women's lives in sports.

This book allows the reader the rare opportunity to hear the stories and viewpoints of 80 female athletes across New England, and 16 female coaches from across the U.S., as well as dozens of informal conversations with male and female soccer coaches, state administrators, and experts from all echelons of the soccer world in the U.S. These detailed stories reveal a gendered world within athletics that is truly paradoxical, for it is both inspiring and invigorating, all while being a contested cultural terrain, where women and young girls fight to have their voices truly heard and validated.

War and Cleats

I first came to this world of soccer through what Lofland and Lofland would call "[starting] where you are," (1995, p.3) as I was first the quintessential, ubiquitous soccer mom. My oldest son Kieran seemed to grow up with a soccer ball attached to his left foot. He played in our town recreation league when he was an elementary school kid racing past kids twice his size. He seemed to love everything about the grass and the goal. Later, upon placing him in a four-day summer camp for school-aged kids at a nearby university, his world really opened up to youth athletics. One sunny afternoon, I left home early to perch myself on the side of the field for the last 30 minutes of camp. It was during this time that the boys were divided up on the grass field, perched under the looming athletic buildings and dorms of the D1 university. I kicked my black sandals off, tucked my toes into the grass, and beamed as I watched my skinny nine-year-old pounding down the field. I didn't recognize any kids or other parents, so the afternoon was delightfully mine to relish. A few minutes later, a tall, lean blond male approached me, hand stretched out to shake mine, saying, "Hi, you must be Kieran's mom?" I told him I was, and we talked about Kieran's drive, tenacity, and love of the game. Chris[1], the coach for the camp and—completely unbeknownst to me, the newbie soccer mom—the head coach for the local men's university soccer team, told me that he also was the director of a local soccer club, Beechwood Soccer, that had tryouts in several weeks. He encouraged me to take Kieran to the tryout day, and headed back to direct the boys in their end-of-the-day match.

---

[1] Names have been changed to protect confidentiality. In addition, I have kept quotations from the interviews in their original format. In doing so, I left grammatical errors in some sentences, but I have chosen to keep the original language as intact as possible in order to respect their normal speaking voices.

Several years later, we found ourselves fully ensconced in the Beechwood club soccer scene, where I eventually took on roles as team manager and eventually vice president of the board of directors. I had entered into a world where both my son and our family would make lifelong friends and meet remarkable women and men. It was during my time working on the Beechwood Soccer Club Board of Directors that a newly hired director of coaching (DOC) asked me, given my expertise as a gender specialist, to help the club figure out why the club was losing girls within the U17 and U18 age groups. The club administrators wanted to know whether the gender attrition was due to club dynamics, regional or national dynamics, or just to the girls themselves? That one question from the DOC ("Will you help us figure this out?") eventually led to this book.

Back in the winter of 2014, I threw myself into my task. We created a working committee on gender issues within the club, comprised of players, coaches, the director of coaching, and myself (a member of the board of directors and a gender consultant). We spent eighteen months strategizing about what was going well for girls within the club, and what was not so positive and needed to be changed. What impressed me the most was that it did not take long for the girls to really embrace and take ownership of the process of investigating gender issues within this committee.

Very shortly after initiating these meetings, it became utterly clear that the players had lots to share, but I wasn't sure if the rest of the girls in the club (ages 8-18) would concur with this select group of players' thoughts, feelings, and experiences. I decided, with approval from the director of coaching, to engage in focus groups with all-female teams at the club in order to assess if the other girls had similar views and experiences. I was completely enamored with (and troubled by) the stories the middle school and high school girls shared with me during those focus group meetings. It was less than a year later, after hearing me talk animatedly and repeatedly about the issues, that my closest friend and colleague encouraged me to expand these interviews to collegiate athletes and coaches.

As of May 2017, I have interviewed 96 soccer individuals between the ages of 11 and 56. I categorize these 96 respondents into three age/life categories: 56 middle and high school players (ages 11–21), 24 collegiate athletes (ages 18–21), and finally 16 female head collegiate coaches (ages 25–56). The student-athletes were all from New England, while the coaches were from twelve states, spanning the country.[2] The formal qualitative interviews (focus groups, face-to-face interviews, and tape-recorded phone interviews) were all completed between May 2014 and May 2017. Dozens of additional informal conversations with soccer state administrators, female and male club coaches, and one gender legal expert were simultaneously collected during that time period.

My work reveals that playing soccer is quite complicated, not in the manner of play, but in the structural dynamics that influence one's presence and experience within the sport. Hundreds of hours of face-to-face interviews, focus groups, and phone interviews have exposed a male-dominated world of soccer

---

2   I should note that the collegiate athletes were from Division II and Division III schools only, while the 16 coaches were from a broad mix of Divisions I, II, and III institutions. Eight coaches were Div. III, five were Div. II, and three were Div. I. The administrators were from all over the country, but primarily the east, west, and central U.S.

rife with a wide continuum of treatment for women: some very positive and productive, some with microinequities (see Mary Rowe 1974), and some with outright discrimination[3]. Thus, I show that the soccer world often becomes a chilly climate, to use Roberta Hall and Bernice Sandler's (1982) term that exposed how women and men are often treated differently in educational environments by both male and female authority figures. My work in contrast looks at how women navigate the gendered, cultural climate of sport, particularly soccer, 36 years later. Some researchers such as Dr. Kitsy Dixon (2014) have argued that qualitative work is the best way to investigate such chilly terrains. Most historical work on the chilly climate shows how men and women are often at odds against each other, yet my work brings new findings to light. My work, in contrast, shows that although women battle with male counterparts for economic and spatial resources, they also utilize male networks carefully and critically to survive in the soccer world. In addition, my work resonates with that of Dixon's by showing that these female soccer coaches sometimes lack female allies within their workplaces. My work exposes that in some cases newly hired female coaches have little to buttress their gender isolation and yet they soldier on, literally and figuratively, because they so badly want young women to not have the same experiences they did. They stay in coaching, even despite the hardships, because they want to make it right or different. It is their vocation, their calling, that keeps them on the athletic fields and in various institutions despite the difficulties.

---

3   Rowe argued that such inequities are the "minutiae of sexism". She noted that such minutiae are "usually not actionable; most are such petty incidents that they may not even be identified, much less protested. She argues they are important though, "like the dust and ice in Saturn's rings, because taken together, they constitute formidable barriers" (1974, 1). She argues that the term is an extension of microaggression theory, which I address later on in this book.

I should note that in terms of difficulties, the Division II and III coaches appeared to talk more about this isolation in a variety of ways than the Div. I coaches, who focused less on their struggles in our conversations. (From here on out I designate such coaches and their divisions by D1, D2, and D3.) That is not to say, however, that the journeys of D1 coaches were conflict-free, it is just that they emphasized discord less often in their interviews than their D2 and D3 counterparts. I am not sure if this was due to their ages, longer work experience, or greater access to resources and capital in their D1 institutions. Future research could, and should, investigate divisional differences amongst female coaches.

My work finds that this chilly climate doesn't freeze women out, but rather toughens them within a new environment, exposing them to new challenges, defeats, and successes. Women have entered into this magical sport, yet I wondered what their experiences were once they were actually part of the soccer team or staff. This book is unique because it is the first major work detailing the hidden stories and experiences of women in the field of American soccer ranging in ages from 11–56.

We have made huge strides in women's sports in the United States in the last decade. The United States Women's National Team (USWNT) won the World Cup in July 2015; just eight months later, however, the USWNT sued U.S. Soccer, claiming they were unfairly discriminated against, given their unequal pay for equal work[4]. Shortly after that, we saw a record number

---

4   Grant Wahl notes that in April 2017, the USWNT reached a collective bargaining agreement (CBA) that provides: "a significant increase in direct compensation and bonus compensation; enhanced 'lifestyle' benefits for the players with respect to travel and hotels; per diems that are equal to those of the men's team;

of female athletes (292 out of 555) from the U.S. attending the Olympic games in Rio De Janeiro, Brazil in 2016. This U.S. female delegation was the largest number of female athletes from one country that had ever competed for a single country ("U.S. sending record number," 2016). During these same Olympics, Simone Manuel became the first African-American female individual gold medalist in swimming. Yet, the women's Olympic successes were often not fully recognized and applauded by all. Saba Mirsalari (2016) recounts what she calls "sexism and gender bias," noting that *NBC* announcers were talking about the U.S. women's gymnastics team as "a group of girls in a mall," in addition to Aly Raisman's makeup. Back in the States, there were similar troubling public statements. Mirsalari mentions the troubling *Chicago Tribune* Twitter feed blunder in which they stated that the United States had won a bronze medal in women's trap shooting, but only mentioned the Olympic medalist as being "the wife of a Bears lineman," initially leaving out her full name, Corey Cogdell-Unrein ("Wife of Bears Lineman," 2016). *New York Times* writer, Katie Rogers, agrees that the coverage was sexist—she also recounts the Cogdell-Unrein issue—and adds how a Texas newspaper headlined Michael Phelps' silver medal victory, while relegating Katie Ledecky's remarkable, world-breaking swim to a smaller font below the Phelps headline on the page (Rogers, 2016). Rogers also points out the ignorance of *BBC* host John Inverdales when he asked tennis star Andy Murray how it felt to be the first person to win two Olympic tennis gold medals, despite the Williams' sisters four Olympic gold medals each (Rogers, 2016). It seemed that while women were making

---

and greater financial support for players who are pregnant and players adopting a child. The separate wage discrimination complaint filed in 2016 by five U.S. players with the Equal Employment Opportunity Commission, remains in place" (Wahl, 1, 2017).

significant impact in sports history in Rio, their full and complete stories were being obfuscated and, in some ways, ignored.

If these women, at the top echelons of professional and Olympic sport aren't being heard, validated, and recognized as full athletes, what happens to other women—middle school, high school, and collegiate athletes? What are their experiences? How do they fare, out of the spotlight and beyond the pages of global newspapers? What about Meggie, the bright-eyed, blonde 12-year-old who has been playing under her father's coaching since she was six years old. She likes soccer, but doesn't love it. She wants to play just for fun, but her father expects otherwise. Her dad already talks about college ID camps, while she can barely think about her test tomorrow on African countries and capitals in her global social studies unit. Her father's silence on car rides home after games leaves her feeling empty and alone. Or how about Leia, the high-schooler from northern New England, who, during the cold, winter months, does homework in the backseat of her mother's Jeep Cherokee on the 40-minute car ride between her indoor club soccer center and indoor lacrosse practice in a different town forty minutes from home. How do these and millions of other female athletes feel about playing a sport? How do they understand their identity in light of their athletic ability? Similarly, what about Melanie, the 37-year-old coach who has finally entered the head coaching office on a beautiful campus nestled out west? Her female Athletic Director (AD) gives her little advice, and even less support. Who will she turn to for advice and support? Or what about Margaret, young and hopeful in her first season as a head coach, but feeling isolated without many other female colleagues in the department to give her guidance and assistance? Her isolation lingers like the winter snow on the trees outside her office window. How will she survive her first season, let alone the rest? How are their experiences different from more seasoned coaches who have been in the sport for much longer? How does sport shape their respective visions, experiences, and ultimately their overall identities as women in 2019?

During the early research process, when I would tell strangers or acquaintances that I was studying young female athletes, several would often guffaw or make critical comments about how hard it must be to talk with teenage girls. I found such comments hateful, cruel, demeaning, and ignorant. Today in America there is a perception that teenage girls are catty, rough, and often exhibit a Queen Bee syndrome by which they are unkind and often territorial in their social behaviors (Derks 2015, Krawcheck 2016)[5]. People make the assumption that girls do not help other girls, and that in doing so, create massive drama throughout their middle school years.

In fact, I even encountered such narrow-minded views with individuals who worked with youth in the soccer world. In the fall of 2015, I had the opportunity to meet a prominent sports writer on youth sports. I had anticipated his presentation as he is highly regarded in the sports world. As the date approached, I was crestfallen when my youngest son became ill and I wasn't sure if I could make the talk. The director of coaching at the club where the meeting was to be held, heard about my predicament, and offered for me to come to an earlier session that would have the

---

5   I should note that some authors even argue that this Queen Bee syndrome exists among middle-aged and professional women. Sallie Krawcheck, former CEO of Merrill Lynch Wealth Management and Smith Barney, notes in a May 23, 2016 Fortune.com article that women can't advance properly in business at times, as there is a queen bee, who is a "senior woman who doesn't help other women advance, who may even actively kick the ladder out from under her when she reaches a top job" (http://fortune.com/2016/05/23/sallie-krawcheck-helping-women/).

same talk, but just with coaches (who happened on that evening to be all men), so I would not have to leave my son home alone at night. I approached the evening with such excitement that I arrived twenty minutes early and took a seat in the second row. Given the empty auditorium, the sports writer immediately came up and introduced himself, and we engaged in about five minutes of light banter about parenting, our children's respective sports interests, and my work in gender and soccer. My feelings of elation, however, were short-lived. As the evening wore on, I realized he had little to no interest in substantive gender issues and I was horrified when he showed a video on intrusive parenting at a soccer match, in which an indifferent mother wildly chatted on her phone, paying little attention to her child. Now, the video in and of itself was nothing we hadn't all seen before, but it was this nationally known author's derisive comment at the end that horrified me. He turned to the audience laughing and said, "Yeah, she's like a cheerleader on crack!" I couldn't believe my ears, so I asked him "What did you say?" He repeated the comment, to the chuckles of the all-male coaching audience.

Later, in his question-and-answer time, I was afraid to ask any questions, feeling so awkward in the environs. I did timidly raise my hand and say (I should note, sadly, in a very stereotypical, deferential female way), "I really appreciate the tools you have given us to put in our toolboxes, really helpful, but I'm wondering what differences you have noticed amongst male and female athletes in your research?" I waited. His response (fumbling in his bag, I should add) was, "Yeah, I have a slide here somewhere on that, I just didn't put it up." He put up a slide showing that girls like to work in pairs, while boys prefer to work alone. Then he added how he had recently called a national coach to get some advice on one of his own girls' team. The author told

20

the audience that the colleague's response was "How old are they? Oh geez, just do whatever you can to get by." Again, the male coaches laughed at the anecdote. I, the only woman in the room, sat there wondering if I had really just witnessed what I thought had taken place. I was stupefied and downtrodden, as he seemed to be saying that girls and women were hard to manage. If he, an acclaimed and esteemed sports expert, attributed such characteristics to girls, what would a less knowledgeable, less informed individual say or believe? He, too, had played out the trope of female athletes as irrational, unstable, emotionally unbalanced individuals.

Unfortunately, it is not just men who play into this gender narrative. Karen Coffin, in her 2009 *Coaching Quarterly* article on coaching girls, says coaches must be prepared, like the Boy Scouts, but then she adds, "stock up on your antacids" (p. 4). She goes on to say that girls will bring "emotions and worries to practice" (p. 5), and that "many a coach has been blindsided when relationships wreck team spirit or players fail to fulfill their potential due to emotional blocks" (p. 4). Too many times we hear about women's negative actions within sports, as opposed to their positive attributes.

What I've realized in the last three years of working on these issues is that these young women and coaches do not typically follow this well-worn trope. In fact, the young girls and women I've met over the past three years are not bitter, petty, and focused on infighting. Rather, they are dynamic, vivacious, energetic, and determined athletes, who just happen to be female. They want to be recognized as being talented, diligent, and successful. The ways they accomplish these goals, however, are shaped by their ages, positions, and social locations.

In chapter 2, I show how middle and high school players have an intense competitive spirit and distinct perceptions of gender inequalities, coupled with acute multilayered parental pressures. I explore two distinct facets of their soccer identity: game face and girl face. The game faces represent the external, public gender inequalities and perceptions that girls articulate regarding their status and experiences within the club in comparison to male players. By contrast, girl faces reflect the private, deeply hidden pressures and struggles they feel, which are rarely discussed within soccer communities. It turns out that girls in the U.S. are facing huge pressures from parents, peers, and ultimately from themselves to excel, be successful, and achieve athletic excellence, all while earning high grades and being involved in all levels of middle and high school extracurricular activities. Such a pressure cooker existence is making them stressed and pressured on and off the soccer field. I should note that one limitation in my research is that it would have been helpful to interview these youngsters' club coaches, both female and male. Such interviews might have brought a broader analysis to the data. I chose not to do these interviews as I wanted the coach information to really focus on female collegiate coaching experiences, and I was afraid that adding in club coach information would cloud the analysis by creating tangents related to pay-to-play models and club politics in youth sports, as well as economic growth battles amongst clubs in various states. Future research on such club issues would be valuable, however, in a broader conversation about gender and sport.

In chapter 3, I expand the analysis to include the parental role in sport. I examine the often hidden strategies "feminist" parents, and particularly fathers, utilize to influence their female daughters' athletic experiences and success within competitive club soccer. To an external observer, these dads are the epitome of modern fathers: coaching their daughters from a young age, encouraging them to excel in an often male-dominated sport, and pushing them to be tough, aggressive, and strong, all while striving for the highest levels of athletic success. However, my research shows that, ironically, this invested parenting is incredibly positive and valuable, yet also challenging and stressful for their daughters. The strategies the parents use range from overt resolute verbal control (from both mothers and fathers) to a variety of forms of covert non-communicative behavior including the silent treatment, socio-emotional pressures, and layers of masked structural control (most often employed by fathers). I explore the multilayered complexity of these parenting strategies, revealing how the daughters feel stifled and hindered by such behavior, while simultaneously appreciating and valuing their parents' lengthy time commitment and financial investment in their athletic endeavors. It is pertinent to acknowledge that this chapter could have as easily been written to focus more closely on over-invested moms, but I chose to emphasize dads, as their experiences in relationship to gender and parenting often don't get as much attention as that of mothers. I was also writing this chapter soon after my aforementioned encounter with the sports writer and I think that probably influenced my decision to focus on dads.

In chapter 4, I shift my focus to 24 D2 and D3 collegiate female players in a conference north of the Mason-Dixon Line. These women play at what is considered the highest level of amateur sport. The experiences of these athletes, however, are far from simple. These student-athletes earn a positive identity marker on campus, and develop incredibly strong bonds with teammates whom they call family, yet there is a negative side to the experience. They face microaggressions of gender insults and gender invalidations in which they are perceived as "just girls," second-class citizens, or "others," if you will. In addition, they face being marked as sexualized objects by their male counterparts and classmates, and face vast inequalities within athletic departments in terms of power, resources, and status. Such findings leave the women perplexed as to why such inequity exists. What is interesting in my findings is that they often deem such inequality as simply societal and in many ways don't like to hone in on gender as a specific variable in their own lives. In fact, they would rather gender not play into the equation of their lives, particularly in that they don't like being called female athletes. They believe gender shouldn't matter, and thus I call them f/athletes, to designate their desire for non-gender-focused identity while continuing to recognize that gender does ultimately matter.

Their stories illuminate the fact that Title IX did not eliminate gender inequity at the collegiate level in a simplistic fiat, and that these women struggle with gender opportunities where supposedly they can be and do anything. My work raises interesting questions about what service we have done to girls (at a young age) by telling them they can be everything. I argue that we must keep giving them those messages, coupled with in-depth conversations about gender inequality, so that they don't reach college with a frustrated sense of structural gender patterns.

I should note here that I am well aware that it would have been helpful to increase my collegiate respondent numbers beyond 24. Unfortunately, I faced incredible difficulty in attempting to do so. It appeared that some teams were too busy to meet during the fall (championship segment) and even later in the spring (out of season or non-championship segment). One D2 female coach was wonderfully receptive, but together we simply couldn't find the right time for me to do the team interviews. Likewise, a D3 male coach was also very kind to me and interested in my work, but I chose not to interview that team due to my own personal connections to the team. Other coaches (male and female) unfortunately were much less receptive, often simply never calling back (despite months of me leaving phone messages) or simply saying that there was absolutely no time in the off season to have me talk with the players. I even attempted to reach one D1 coach for over a year, hoping to interview a sample of her roster, without much luck. This particular coach did call me back at my home number, but never followed up to arrange an actual time for the team interview. Such barriers left me wondering if these coaches were hesitant about people entering into their domain and accessing their players for information. Were they nervous about what I might unearth? Or was it just sheer busyness that kept the silent ones from calling back? I found the avoidance behavior strange as the female coaches were always so willing to meet with me, and be interviewed about their own personal experiences. Interestingly, I had no problems whatsoever finding and interviewing D1, D2, and D3 coaches. In fact, if I could have kept the research going for longer than three years, I could have easily doubled my respondent numbers in terms of female coaches regarding their journeys within soccer. I chose to stop interviewing when I did, in order to finish the manuscript in time for publication prior to the Women's World Cup 2019.

Chapter 5 examines gender and career identity amongst those 16 head female collegiate soccer coaches (D1, D2, D3) from across the United States. Despite vast changes for female soccer players in the United States over the last thirty years (e.g., rapid increase in youth players, successes of U.S. Women's National team, and increased social media coverage about young female athletes), I show that Bernice Sandler's notion of an entrenched chilly climate now exists for women within sports departments: women being devalued, stereotyped, given lower expectations, and facing blatant harassment. What impact can female coaches have upon their athletes while working within such college athletic environs? I reveal how coaches are actively working to reverse negative treatment by exerting vast personal and social influence upon players within three often interlocking dimensions: behavioral, relational/cultural, and professional. In many ways, the coaches are trying to pave a different road for their female athletes, so the athletes can avoid a similar chilly climate in their future endeavors.

Finally in chapter 6, I continue to explore how these same coaches use various strategies within their respective workplaces to survive. Women who eventually become head coaches often find themselves in new job environments with little knowledge of how to navigate their new responsibilities. It is not that they don't know how to play soccer, or that they aren't good at coaching, but that they have never been in collegiate work environments sitting in the head coach's office. Additionally, they look around and see very few women in the hallways and conference rooms of their athletic departments. Thus, they find themselves in a unique situation: well-trained and professionally poised to begin their head coach careers and yet somewhat isolated in these new environs. My research shows that women subsequently engage in four main strategies for navigating their new terrain: attempting to create new allies within their athletic departments, relying upon male mentors (most often male coaches encountered earlier in their career arc), fighting back against the sexism, and finally, in a very few cases, retreating or quitting.

What is unique from the findings in this chapter is that many of the coaches I met engaged in cross-gender mentoring with males, as there were few women to support them in some environments. Such mentoring is not unique, as it is often found in the business world, but what is different is that these soccer coaches turned to males outside their work environments, unlike their female business counterparts. They turned to former coaches and mentors who, in some cases, now lived hundreds of miles away. Such long distance mentoring was used for job planning, emotional support, and procedural support. They often spoke so highly of these male mentors that they eventually became friends and, in some cases, like family to them. Such effective e-mentoring may have strong, positive implications for women outside sport as a model within isolated work environments.

The second way that women tried to survive in male-dominated environments as head coaches was by trying to build ally networks with male and female colleagues. In some cases, the women found supportive, helpful allies in their male team coaches who offered new perspectives and a listening ear. But too often, they found themselves battling male egos and patriarchy. One coach was called "princess" by her male athletic director, while another had a clipboard thrown at her head by her male AD. Such discrimination, although rare in my data, shows that unfortunately women are up against a difficult male terrain. One wonders how many other women face such treatment. Some coaches also found helpful and positive support in their sparsely numbered female colleagues, but in a few cases they faced the Queen Bee syndrome of female ADs that did little to support or guide their new female hires.

The final strategies were women looking outside the university for support, in one case taking legal action, and in some cases where they felt little support, some women contemplated quitting their jobs. Such findings are sad and disheartening, given how valuable we see these women being to the younger generation.

As I mentioned earlier, there are always limitations when writing a book, and another one here was the lack of male voices. I specifically chose not to add formal male interviews in my research framework as I believed they would have obfuscated the focal point of the women's experiences. However, in saying that, I recognize that men's voices in female sport need to be heard and should be included in future research. I think that these male voices could be really valuable particularly in terms of future discussions about collaboration and mentorship. We often see people arguing that girls need to be supported by female role models, and yet I propose that female mentors should also be mentoring young boys. Dr. Niobe Way's (2016) research on young boys' development shows that young men benefit from the skills that older female mentors bring to a cross-gendering relationship. I believe that such "flipped" mentoring could help young boys see and connect to female role models long before they take on traditional gender beliefs in their teenage years about role models and gender.

In addition, I am cognizant that the majority of my respondents are white. This demographic fact was not by design, but simply a reality as my research unfolded. I used a snowball sample and when I asked coaches to recommend a friend or two, their recommendations just happened to be white individuals. Moreover, it should be noted that when I collected quantitative data (with the help of an undergraduate student of mine) on coaching staff across the United States, we were shocked at how white the rosters of D1, D2, and D3 female soccer teams were in 2017. Beyond our data, it would be valuable for future research to explore both why few racial minority women play collegiate soccer, and in turn, what their specific experiences are in comparison to their white teammates.

Looking ahead to the future, it appears that female athletes will continue to grow in number, yet one wonders what the expectations and experiences of the next crop of young athletes will be. The final chapter concludes with the idea that we must focus on more ongoing qualitative data to better understand the experiences of players and coaches within soccer in America today, if we are to retain these newest, youngest players within this beautiful game. I offer up solutions to deal with the extensive gender inequality that these young women and coaches delineate in the earlier chapters. First, I return to GO BEECHWOOD (outlined specifically in chapter 2) as a model to examine how such bottom-up, athlete-led models might be useful for various clubs around the country. Models like Go Beechwood may, in fact, be the place where we not only enable girls to find their voices off the field, but also a place where they can have in-depth conversations about gender inequity and sexism. Such spaces are critical for young girls (and all of us) in this current, volatile gender climate in 2019.

I also address solutions to parental pressures in this concluding chapter. I posit that more parents should actually get involved in club board work in order to truly see what happens off the field in various facets of youth sport. Boards tend to be male driven and male dominated and yet I argue that if we had more women (and men who want to focus on their daughters' experiences) flooding boards with their respective skills, we might find more solutions for young female athletes.

I also argue that with more women entering boards, we might find more ways for greater gender collaboration within clubs.

Such collaborative efforts are not only a hugely positive step for creating change, but are a wonderful model for young girls showing that feminist change can happen alongside gender-aware men in sports. I argue that we must show young girls that *all males* are not the problem in the world today, instead pointing out the positive older male mentors that many female coaches rely strongly upon.

Finally, I argue that we must look to female coaches as a model for stamping out the Queen Bee syndrome in the world today. We must use their examples to view how and why they don't let female rivalry and competition stop their collaborative efforts. In turn, their experiences will help us further e-mentoring as a positive model for women in many other fields.

Beyond these chapters, appendix I provides an additional reading list of sociology research that speaks to specific themes within this book. First, I detail the pivotal pieces within the general literature on women and soccer, and then turn my attention to literature that relates specifically to female athletes. In this category I highlight material on injury prevention, player performance, and valuable work on the gender athlete paradox. Finally, in the last section of this appendix, I summarize the material related to female coaches. The topics in this last category focus on inequality and sexual discrimination, attitudes and perceptions of coaches, and a few titles that explore homophobia in the experiences of female coaches. This reading list is in no way meant to be exhaustive, but simply is a tool for further reading on gender and sport, if desired.

Turning back to my own research, some might say that what my work ends up revealing is that women simply want to have a voice, and that is certainly true. Yet, this book shows that there is more to the equation than that. These young girls and older women are actively concerned with the opposite of the petty stubborn jealous woman trope. In fact, they are working on what I see as transformative sports virtues. These soccer women in every age category and corner of this country are trying to be part of a historically male-dominated sport that often hasn't found a space or voice for them. Most Americans see them on the town greens and in recreation parks, but don't know what or who they really are, and what they really are about. This book reveals that we have to look a lot more intently, and often beyond the soccer field to see what their true, full ambitions are.

In many ways, my opportunity to meet and have in-depth conversations with these 96 women exposed that their goals are often akin to the meaningful metrics that David Brooks wrote about in his *New York Times* editorial "The Moral Bucket List" (April 11, 2015). He argues that people either have resume or eulogy virtues. The resume virtues are what he calls "the skills you bring to the marketplace," while the eulogy virtues are those that are talked about at your funeral..."whether you were kind, brave, honest, or faithful" (p. 1). He notes that society expects us to have the former, but he believes we should be worrying about the latter. Brooks' notion of what is truly meaningful hits home here as I think about gender and sport as well. Brooks argues that there are six components or experiences that one should have on the way to the "richest possible inner life" (p. 2). What is remarkable to me is that the women I met (from middle school to middle age) held on tightly to four of these characteristics: recognition of dependency, the need to be brave, understanding a vocation, and finally having what Brooks calls "an energizing love" (p. 4). The girls and coaches, first and foremost, recognized that they had not reached their levels of sport alone because, as Brooks says, "people on the road to character understand that no person can achieve self-mastery on his or her own" (p. 3). These women recognized their dependency upon others and valued those relationships deeply.

Second, Brooks notes that fulfilled people recognize they must "crash through the barriers of their fears" (p. 6). The soccer women I met did just that. They knew whether they were battling fears about their parents' expectations, taking on cultural battles about what it means to be athletic and female, or the uncertainty of the demands in a new job, that they must face their uneasiness and battle it head on.

Third, the women, particularly the coaches, understood the "call within the call" (p. 5), as Brooks puts it. These women knew that their jobs were more than just jobs, they were a calling. Brooks argues that "all that matters is living up to the standard of excellence inherent in their craft" (p. 5). The women I met did just that; they strove to live up to a standard of excellence, not only for themselves, but as an example for those who came after them.

Finally, the women exhibit another of Brooks' traits of eulogy virtues, which is an "energizing love," (p. 4) which he argues decenters the self, allowing us to recognize that there is more than our self-centered being. Brooks argues that such a love reminds us that "our true riches are in another" (p. 5). This is truly what I found about these athletes. Their glory and belief went beyond themselves to the team. They knew that they were always working together for the good (and betterment) of the whole, every step of the way. They were not in it for the aggrandizement of self, but rather for the sum of the parts.

They strive, pursue, and aspire to be soccer athletes at the highest levels, whether that be on the field, in the coaching office, or behind an administrator or state association desk, yet in doing their jobs (and, I should add, doing them well) many of them chose not to focus on gender in their experiences. I wasn't sure if that was because they often didn't have the opportunity to talk about these issues or if it was a purposeful choice to not focus on gender influences in their experiences. Some of the respondents even vacillated about how important gender as a variable even was; they argued that gender did not matter, all while relaying examples of subtle, and not so subtle, inequality.

I think in many ways these athletes weren't sure how to process the gender piece, as they didn't want to believe that gender mattered as much as it did. They wanted to believe that they could play with the boys, as most had done as kids, and that they were in fact equal. They wanted to remain steadfast in their belief that they were *as good, as talented,* and *as successful* as their male colleagues. Admitting any less would be seen as failure.

What became evident during the data collection process was that they had thought about these issues for a long time in their own minds, but had rarely been asked to discuss and parse out their thoughts. Not many people had ever asked them what it meant to be female in this contested space or how things might be best, given their unique positions. Thus, the interviews became a slow trickle of viewpoints and visions that got pieced together over time.

I give you their stories, their voices. I cannot thank them all enough for sharing their intimate, and at times vulnerable, experiences. I am honored to have listened to, and been entrusted with, their life histories and intertwined athletic journeys. They have certainly enriched my own feminist journey and for that I am eternally grateful to each and every one of them. What I bring to their analysis is small in comparison to what they bring to this sport, which is often called the world's most beautiful game.

Chapter 2

Girl Face vs. Game Face: Deciphering Middle and High School Girls' Experiences in Beechwood Soccer Club[6]

Returning to the introduction of this book, more and more girls are playing soccer in America, yet what do we know about the time these youngsters spend in training sessions with their teammates?[7] The numbers of female athletes is skyrocketing; yet these soccer clubs still have administrators, board presidents, and coaches that are often predominantly male. While Lopez (1997), Kooistra (2005), Jeanes (2011), and Welford (2011) all examine

---

6   Originally published by Common Ground Research Networks in the *Journal of Sport and Health*, Volume 6, Issue 4. All Rights Reserved. Permissions: support@cgnetworks.org.
        Bhave, Maya, and James Franklin. 2016. "Collaboration, Gender Differences, and the Go Nordic Model: Eliciting Social Change within One New England Soccer Club." *Journal of Sport and Health* 6 (4): 13-29. http://doi.org/10.18848/2381-7070/CGP/v06i04/13-29.

7   It is important to note that although this chapter focuses on primarily white players within a New England community there are concomitant patterns of increased soccer involvement in a variety of predominantly racial minority communities across the United States. (See USSF research by Ed Foster-Simeon on Soccer for Success Programs, 2013)

how females are entering the sport and changing the external look of soccer, there is a significant dearth of literature on how they fare once on the team.

As I mentioned in chapter 1, I was involved in club soccer at a personal level as a parent, team manager, and later as a board of director's member. Yet I had no idea my investment in youth soccer was soon going to get much more complicated, as it quickly evolved into professional research in early January 2014. This chapter examines the findings of that research with middle and high school female players. Working with the director of coaching (from hereafter called the DOC) of the travel soccer club, and building upon Ruth Jeanes' work (2011, p. 405), we set out to examine how gender was constructed in fluid, dynamic ways within the club. Together we wanted to know why girls were dropping out within the older cohorts, and particularly if this was something unique to this club. The DOC and I started with the principal idea that the female experience needed to be fully explored, and we wanted to investigate how female athletes were doing socially, emotionally, and physically in this club, which had primarily male administrators and board of directors.

The data I collected reveals answers to that multilayered question within this one soccer club and illuminates the intricacies of why girls enter soccer, what they need and expect when they are there, and what societal and parental pressures they face. The findings show that girls (1) want to be challenged similarly to boys, (2) need coaches who understand their experiences, and (3) face intense (often unspoken) pressures from societal norms and often their own parents. My research shows how female athletes engage in constructing identities based upon public versus private personas, specifically external identities—what

I call game faces—versus their internal struggles—their girl faces. I reveal how these athletes desperately want public equity in terms of training, opportunities, expectations, and status, while simultaneously struggling privately with the intense pressures of being "uber" teenage girls who are successful at all levels. I show how such struggles are always under the surface and subsequently impact their public athletic endeavors every time they get dropped off for a practice or walk onto the field. Such multilayered findings on teenage gender identity and pressure are critical to deconstruct and explore if American youth soccer is going to survive. If such findings are obscured or ignored, I believe that we will see a broader attrition crisis among American female athletes, at least in youth soccer.

RESEARCH PROCESS

Between February 2014 and December 2014, I used two primary types of qualitative methodological practices (group interview data through formal focus groups with 48 players, coupled with oral data from a gender working committee) to examine the fluid, complex nature of gender at Beechwood Soccer Club[8]. I should note that an additional 8 interviews were done later in 2015 with middle school athletes who were not included in this first round, thus bringing the final total to 56 middle school and high school respondents. First, in order to get a clearer sense of what was happening at the club, the DOC created a working committee on gender in February 2014, whose sole purpose was to explore what we were doing well for our female players within the club and what

---

8   All names have been changed to protect the confidentiality of the respondents, as was stated in permission forms given to and signed by parents.

needed to be strengthened. The DOC and I chose the committee members together, which was comprised of one board member, the DOC, two coaches of female teams, and several female players. Later we constructed focus group questions in order to determine if the gender findings from the committee were congruous for girls aged 11-18 across the whole club, and finally a gender initiative, called GO BEECHWOOD, was developed and implemented, as a response to the social science data I had collected.

The changes at Beechwood Soccer are unique because they happened from the bottom up within a collaborative model where the club administrators listened to the voices of the players before making any programmatic changes. This approach is often not the method used in male-run soccer clubs across the globe (see Welford, 2011), where top administrators simply implement new programs and initiatives with little player input (see Borden, Eder, Williams & Harress, 2014). Our research framework was grounded in applied sociology practices and subsequently elicited precise, scientific data.

This project, structured by co-investigators with different skill sets and gender perspectives, fostered collaboration and learning from each other, and cultivated a broad impact across the club[9]. One might immediately question if two internal administrators from the club had any insider advantages, thus creating any

---

9   Such a framework is unique in gender-focused projects in soccer environments, as often it is solely women who are responsible for making gender changes (see Fielding-Lloyd and Mean, 2011). My work with the male DOC proved valuable at many levels; not only did he share valuable soccer knowledge and insights about sport in general, but his male perspective gave our research validity with other male administrators.

limitations in the research. The answer is that, while being insiders did allow us easy access to databases of rosters, player schedules, and email lists, this did not skew our data findings. On two occasions, our process was actually questioned—not because we were insiders, but because certain board members, and a few parents felt that such a gender undertaking appeared inequitable for the male players. Such findings reflect Caudwell's findings (2003) which show that when women, bodies, gender, and sex are analyzed within football clubs, the gender order is disturbed, thus troubling various constituents (pp. 376-377). Fielding-Lloyd and Mean's findings (2011) show that boundaries in sport are often constructed in a way to resist change (p. 346).

Looking beyond gender, most of our respondents were white and middle class, and yet our research pairs nicely as an accompaniment to the work of Annette Lareau (2011). Lareau's work compares frenetic middle-class families' focus on "concerted cultivation" (p. 2)—a framework by which parents strive to teach children the world through vast opportunities and organized activities—to working class families, who focus more on what she calls "the natural growth of development process" (p. 2). Her work on how middle class family lives are structured solely around their entitled children's lives is extremely valuable, yet she fails to get at the underpinnings of how these middle class children feel and subsequently react to their frenetic worlds. My research remedies that gap by gleaning those often hidden, unspoken reactions. As such, my work also resonates clearly with Erving Goffman's (1959) historic work on the presentation of self, regarding front and back stages, as I explicitly detail both the public and private faces of these young, female athletes' lives.

FIRST STEPS: WORKING COMMITTEE FINDINGS

The working committee had very little data to begin with, primarily anecdotal evidence and attrition numbers (figure 1).

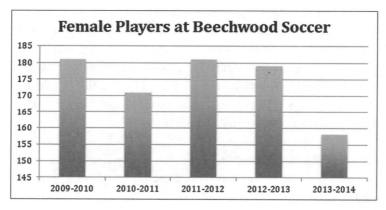

Figure 1

We knew that national data showed that girls started sports later and dropped out sooner than boys, and that rural girls had higher dropout rates than suburban girls, but lower rates than urban girls (Sabo & Veliz, pp.125-132). We wondered if we were reproducing these patterns in our club, or whether something unique was happening within Beechwood Soccer.

Concerned about the radical drop in female players in 2013-2014, we asked the players on the committee to describe the female experience at Beechwood. Girls' responses revealed they wanted to be treated equally to boys, and often struggled with coaches who were too nice or wouldn't give them valuable criticism. These girls wanted, first and foremost, to excel as players; they valued their time on the field and wanted it to stand for something. Charlotte, a player from the oldest cohort, spoke in one of our very first gender committee meetings about females' intense competitive drive, stating definitively, "We want coaches to push us to win, like the boys' coaches do. Not just help us. We don't want coaches to just be nice." It is important to note that other girls echoed these same sentiments in later focus groups.

When asked to reflect on strengths at the club, they noted social relationships between teammates as the key strength, followed by kindness despite team losses and overall strong chemistry between players, particularly due to the "no captain" framework within the club. Girls felt that having no set captain allowed for more free-flowing leadership roles to emerge. They spoke highly and favorably of this model. Yet, in the same breath, girls noted that there were perceived differences between club and premier[10] teams (which created a hierarchical dissonance and division) and cliques that created exclusion; that there were few female role models and few male coaches who had strong knowledge of gender development and psychology; and that they felt that girls were not getting the same fitness and technical training as the boys (see figure 2). The girls kept referring to the fact that if they were a male player at Beechwood, they would experience soccer quite differently. Paradoxically, however, these frustrations were embedded in an environment that they also cherished due to strong friendship ties.

---

10   At Beechwood Soccer Club, tryouts were held to determine the ability of all players. Athletes of higher skill levels were subsequently placed on A or 1st teams (called premier teams), while the others were placed on B or 2nd teams (called club teams). Such differentiations led to teams attending different tournaments and leagues.

Postive perceptions	Negative perceptions
• Social relationships with teammates • Kindness • Team chemistry • No set captain model	• Club and premier differences • Cliques • Few female role models • Less skill and technical training than boys

Figure 2 Female perceptions of Beechwood Soccer Club

To figure out if this data would be replicated beyond this select group of female players, we arranged seven focus groups with 56 girls total of girls between ages 11-18 (that comprised 33% of our overall female players between the ages of 11-18), structured around the concept of player history within the club[11]. We wanted to decipher why players joined the club; what their views were of teams, player environment, and coaching staff once here; and what they perceived as areas of strengths and weaknesses within the club. The committee decided upon ten formal questions (which had been democratically voted on, and chosen from a larger list of 25 crafted by committee members). Given the qualitative training of the facilitator, the questions were used as a guideline within the broad framework of collecting player histories (see figure 3). These questions framed the girls' experiences, and allowed us to decipher underlying themes and issues that related to the aforementioned literature: what are girls' experiences in these clubs (Lopez); difference and variance in those experiences (Caudwell); how gender is fluidly constructed within context (Jeanes); how girls' focus on intrinsic values

---

11   We chose to interview only girls aged 11 and older as we anticipated it would be difficult to elicit useful gender data from 8-, 9-, and 10-year-olds.

shapes experience (Atkins), and how boys and girls experience sports differently (Milyak).

Figure 3 Focus Group Questions

1. Tell me how you ended up joining Beechwood.

2. Think back on the past year, and tell me what went really well.

3. What didn't go as you had hoped or planned?

4. Do you think boys and girls are treated equally at Beechwood?

5. What pressures do you feel from teammates?

6. What pressures do you feel from coaches?

7. What pressures do you feel from parents or family?

8. What makes you stay at Beechwood?

9. Do you think Beechwood is helping you reach your goals as a player?

10. Would you be interested in more informational meetings, specifically for females, on nutrition, the mental aspect of the game, and physical conditioning and training?

The seven focus groups were held at a neutral site, a classroom at a local private, liberal arts college. This location decreased distractions and allowed the girls privacy away from the indoor soccer facility, while promoting a setting of professionalism. Female respondents for the focus groups were chosen based upon systematic sampling of team rosters. In addition, consent forms were approved by the club administrator and signed by parents, giving girls permission to attend these tape-recorded sessions.

One of the earliest findings in the focus groups was that the majority of the girls were shocked that the club was even investigating gender issues. Some girls were confused as to who might be at the sessions—some worrying that boys might be included—while others felt that it was great to have a place to discuss "girl stuff." One U14 player, Francine, stated:

> It makes you feel accepted and involved. It makes you feel there are people who care about what you feel and your opinions, and you're not just flying under the radar. That you're someone and you can make a difference.

When asked what "flying under the radar" meant, Francine replied,

> You're there, but no one's really noticing you or listening to you. You're going unnoticed...we feel not important...like nothing.

It was Sara, a U16 player, who really summed up the nascent stage of the project:

This is the first time Beechwood has put an effort into talking to the athletes instead of just letting everything be done by the parents and administration. Now it's actually the athletes, which is cool for me.

FINDINGS AND DISCUSSION

The focus group data show that girls engage in distinct gender performativity as athletes publicly and privately, resulting in what we term girl face (internal, hidden feelings and pressure regarding perfection) versus game face (the visible, external inequalities that girls feel are inherent within club)[12]. Our work resonates strongly with Ruth Jeanes' (2011) concept of the *performing girl*, as we too explore how being a girl is played out within the male-dominated organization of Beechwood Soccer Club. Jeanes notes in her work that this new "breed of girl" (p.404) knows what she wants and pursues it; our work moves beyond her definition to show the hidden, often unspoken, ramifications of being a girl in 2019.

These dual personas illuminate the external social inequalities and expectations of girls, coupled with the deeply hidden pains of these seemingly vibrant, dynamic young athletes. It is important to recognize that the girls spoke in detail about each persona, despite the fact that others within the club or their families were not always aware of the girls' feelings or perceptions.

---

12   The term *game face* within American sports typically denotes being ready for game day with an intense, focused demeanor. My term includes such a competitive spirit, yet broadens the term to include all public presentations of self within the club. As such, this term speaks to the vast inequalities the girls saw structurally within the club.

GAME FACE: THE VISIBLE EXTERNAL INEQUALITIES

One early finding of inequality was related to the girls' desire for coaches to recognize their ambitious drive. First and foremost, girls felt that coaches didn't understand they were just as capable as their male counterparts. Jane, a vocal high school player, noted, "We want to be treated more like a male athlete, I guess. Have different practices and different styles." One teammate concurred, "Don't treat us like we have any less of an ability," while another added, "I feel like we should have the same opportunities as the boys." Girls wanted us to hear that they needed to be seen as determined and dedicated, not dainty. Time and time again they spoke about how coaches walk and talk them through drills, as compared to boys' coaches who "show them how to do it and show them at pace how to do it." Amy, a U14 player, said "They challenge the boys more," with her teammate Naomi, adding in agreement, "I feel like they don't want to hurt our feelings." But it was Alicia, a U14 player, who summed up the female competitive drive most clearly:

> Like the boys coaches push them harder, I guess. I guess, they don't want to hurt our feelings, but if they want us to succeed, then they need to know we need discipline, too. We need somebody that when we do something wrong, they're gonna punish us. They need to punish us in a way that's gonna help us get better and improve our game. I'm sorry, but doing five push-ups isn't gonna help a soccer player.

These players wanted the exact same experience and opportunities offered to the boys, and unfortunately, they didn't feel there was equality within the small, tight-knit club. For the most part, they felt that the administrators in the club did not focus on such inequities. In fact, most girls loudly blurted out a definitive "no" before I was even done asking the question about whether the club treated boys and girls equally. Such findings speak to the vast inequities girls often face in male-run organizations (Caudwell, 2011, p.330).

The younger girls at Beechwood, however, saw the inequalities as issues of confidence and innate abilities, tending to focus on gender traits, while the older girls saw the gender differences as structural social inequalities entrenched within the club hierarchy. Kristi, a U12 player, said:

> I think that most of the boys, they have more confidence going into Beechwood than probably the girls do. Because the boys don't really care how people judge them much, but the girls... I don't really like when people judge me, so I'm guessing that no one likes to be judged much, and they don't want to be coming into Beechwood and being really bad at soccer, so that's probably why they choose not to do Beechwood.

Her teammate Mary echoed that sentiment:

> Boys don't have any drama. I don't think they're there to make friends. They're just there to play soccer. Girls want to play soccer, but they want to make friends too. Boys want to make friends too, but it's not like they're so worried about that. Because they [girls] don't want to be alone, they want to be with somebody.

Kristi believed it was their physical stature and style of play that made them different:

> I think the boys' games are a lot more aggressive than girls' games. More boys are probably gonna head the ball than girls. Because they're like, "Oh my God, my head hurts." It does hurt sometimes, and then boys aren't afraid to push someone. We're just like, "Ah, you're my friend, and I don't want to push you."

A U13 player agreed with Kristi's premise about boys and their different manner of playing soccer:

> They don't really care. If they're playing soccer, they're gonna do whatever they can to get that ball. Girls are like that too, but not so much because if they're a friend, they're like, "Aah, not going to."

One phrase that resonated strongly with the younger girls, but never came up with older girls was "you kick like a girl." To these young girls this was the highest insult. When I asked what that meant, they said it involved "toeing it." Many of the younger girls noted that boys used that specific criticism, among others, to demean them. Older girls did not speak of such taunting, which I believe reflects socio-psychological age development differences.

Mary, the U12 player, summed up the younger girls' feelings about gender inequities regarding athletic expectations at this young age:

> Once, our gym teacher had us line up—boys and girls—because she was going to show us the 50-yard dash or something, and this guy goes, "Why do we have to race

the girls? We already know who's gonna win." And I was like, "Sure you do! What the heck?"

It was the older girls, in contrast, who spoke to structural, systemic differences that they felt the club perpetuated, which kept the boys at a "different level than girls." Such attitudes strongly differed from the younger girls, who simply saw boys as different, distinct beings who viewed them as lesser, as "the other." When asked if boys and girls were equal, Jane, a U16 player, had a look of disdain, stating:

> Well, I think some boys' teams have three practices a
> week instead of two. The boys have more opportunities
> to play sometimes, I feel. Well, one example comes to
> my mind. Last year for the Beechwood Tournament,
> the boys were playing—I guess there could have been
> girls teams too, I'm not exactly positive—but I know
> a lot of the boys' teams played at [the local university]
> at the really nice new turf field and we played, I don't
> know where we played. And then one year, we played
> at the lacrosse and football practice field at Telford 3 or
> 4 years ago maybe, while other people—boys—were
> playing on turf, at good fields.

Her teammate added to the conversation around boys' capabilities:

> I don't know their coaches, but I feel like they have
> better coaches. Their success rate is so much higher than
> ours, and they're so much more advanced. Our boys'
> U16 team I feel is so much more advanced than us, just
> as a whole unit.

When pressed to explain what she meant by "advanced," she responded:

> Yeah, like skills and just the way they work together is better. I don't know if that has to do with their coaching, but it just seems like they have more of an advantage. Like they learn more and they benefit more from Beechwood than we do.

The girls felt the club was giving better opportunities to the boys' side. Another U16 player conveyed her view on the coaching inequities between boys' and girls' teams:

> I've also noticed that boys have more consistent coaching. Like a coach will stay with them for almost the whole time they play Beechwood, which I think is really important. Like with our team, we've switched coaches so many times and I think it's hard, because you get used to one coach and then you switch and it's a completely different playing style and you have to start all over again, so it would be awesome if girls could have consistent coaches, because I've noticed that we don't, at all.

Even when given examples of boys' teams that had switched coaches many times, the girls were adamant. They continued to speak with specificity, noting that the boys actually had greater expectations placed upon them by coaches, and thus were given more in return. One older girl, Audrey, noted:

> I think the coaching style for boys and girls is different. Like they're boys and I guess they're better at soccer so

> I feel like they work more on possession and moves and all this stuff, and we're just not as good. Like we don't do possession or anything like that. Because we're just not as skilled.

When asked if boys are really better at soccer, she continued:

> I think it's just like a common, like people think boys are better. Like it's a given. Yeah, like they're stronger and faster and more skilled, and just...better.

This sentiment was met with agreement from around the room. The girls were discerning enough, however, to note that there were nuances in their experiences. They noted that individual coaches, and most importantly team chemistry affected these differences. Jeanne spoke to the bonds built within teams:

> I know that, for guys, it's just so simple for them to make friends and to be just, oh, yeah, you like this, I like that too, we can be friends. For girls it's a lot harder. I think in some ways, we can have stronger opinions and we can clash on the field sometimes, which is hard, and you get annoyed, and then there's tension. But it's all secret, we never really talk to each other about what our issues are. Like if I have a problem with a certain player, I would never say it to them because you're playing on a team with them, you can't really tell them you hate them because I'm gonna be stuck with them so I can't like, be upset with them. They [boys] can be upset, and then they'll be over it a minute later.

They recognize how difficult this is for girls, though. Sara commented:

> I mean, it's kind of too bad. Because I think it would be nice to be able to just say it. Like I look at Jane, just as an example, and I would say, "Jane, you need to try harder." Some girls would take offense to that and hold it against you forever. But guys would just be like, "Oh, okay," and then just get over it in the next couple of minutes. So I think that's kind of unfortunate. Because you should just be able to say it. You're telling them not to be mean, but to benefit the team.

Kim agreed:

> I just feel like guys, they don't really care what they say to each other. Girls just take it to heart and you just need to learn to shake things off, and if someone tells you something on the field, it's to help the team as a whole, and they're not picking you out of the bunch.

Finally, girls felt that the club expected more from the boys than the girls. One U16 player declared:

> I feel they're held to a higher standard and have higher expectations. Like they're expected to win state cup. I feel like if we lose, I feel like they're not necessarily super surprised. But I know when the 15 boys lost, the 16s this year, lost to Brunswick United, everyone was like "What? Nobody beats Beechwood in state cup, what is this?" But I think the year under us got beat, and we're just like, "Oh well." We're just used to it now.

What is fascinating about these data, is that not only did they vary based upon age level of the female player, but they revealed that girls and young women perceived rigid gender inequalities based upon what they saw as inherent societal beliefs that were in turn being perpetuated by club coaches and administrators. My results not only unearthed these strongly held feelings, but revealed a broad, deeply rooted belief of inequality that was not readily evident from trainings that looked—externally anyway—positive, vibrant, and productive. This research in many ways is evidence that what appears to be working well is not always operating in ways that are giving players the most exceptional experience. Deeper investigation of my data, however, revealed other gendered differences, and those were even more troubling.

GIRL FACE: THE PRIVATE PERSONA

In direct contrast to outward, external expectations, my research reveals that girls felt intense internal pressure to be a super or "uber" girl. Unlike the aforementioned structural and physical inequities that varied based upon age, these private struggles crossed all age groupings within Beechwood, and thus were extremely troubling. Interestingly, the girls wanted to talk much more about these girl-face struggles, resulting in about twice as much girl-face data as game-face data. I fully believe this fact reveals that girls often did not have a comfortable venue to discuss these private pressures and thus found the focus groups a safe, confidential setting to discuss such matters.

Girls noted pressures from many areas, but tended to get most emotional talking about their parents. These girls strongly valued their families, yet felt misunderstood in many situations. They recognized that their families helped them get to where they are as athletes, yet that support came at an emotional price for them. The girls spoke intensely about complex feelings over the investment their parents had made. Jane lamented:

> I feel a lot of pressure from one of my parents. If I didn't play, it would be a huge disappointment and I feel like this parent would feel that it's always the money, that I played for so long, and not necessarily that this parent would think of happiness—more like how it affected their life. And like, I thank this parent for everything they've pushed me to do. A lot of the decisions that this parent has made—that I didn't necessarily think I wanted to do—have really helped me and really impacted my game and made things better. But other times, I feel they don't understand where I'm coming from, or don't try to understand. It's really good to have people believe in me and think I can play in college and I should and I want to, but I don't know the capacity that I want to or where I can.

Another girl, Audrey shared her similar dilemma:

> I have big pressure from my parents, especially my dad. Like I feel like they'd get, not mad at me, but they've spent so much money and if I were to just stop, they'd be not angry but frustrated. At the same time, they want me to play college soccer and sometimes I do and sometimes I don't, I haven't decided that, but they keep signing me up for these clinics and I don't know, and they keep pressuring me to email coaches and do all this stuff. I don't know if I want to. I don't want to

go college and spend all my time doing soccer if I don't want to. Because that's what we've been doing in high school.

In addition, many pointed out that their dads played soccer at earlier ages, and thus their criticism was probably justified, as hard as that was.

In direct contrast, some girls disliked that their parents actually knew nothing about sports and felt that their comments were completely useless. One U15 player shared:

> After a game, all my parents will say is, "You tried your hardest, good job." Even if I didn't and even if it wasn't a good job. And sometimes that kind of psychs me out in a bad way. I feel like the fact that my parents aren't sports enthusiasts, so they don't watch sports all the time, they don't watch sports games, even though I have a really athletic brother.

One middle-school player, Sue, noted that her dad comments on her play, even though he has never played the game:

> He thinks he knows all that there is to know about soccer. He says, "I've been watching it longer than you've been playing, so I know more about it." And every single car ride back is like, "Oh, you should have done this better, you should have done this rather than that."

One of Sue's teammates suggested that her parents, also not knowledgeable about soccer, would be more helpful and valid in their criticisms if they studied the sport online before being critical. My research showed that girls wanted constructive criticism, not as one girl put it "a mom who tells me I did well, when I know I didn't."

In addition, I found that girls felt pressured to be perfect on the field, as well as off. This intense drive for perfection—not often discussed in the soccer circles I had been within—was most troubling to me given how young many of these girls are. Georgia, a U15 player, elaborated on the pressures she felt:

> I have to be the best at not only sports but also academics. And they push me and for academics it's really difficult because with honor courses, there's so much homework and papers on top of your regular classes and on top of sports, you have to go all out and above. This isn't necessarily correct for all boys, but I feel, academically, parents expect something different from girls and they expect them to have all As and it's just this idea of perfection that can't really be touched.

Her teammate Chelsea agreed:

> Yeah, it's definitely true. Like boys, they might have other sports but most of them don't really do band or sing, and they don't really have to try to have a social life. They just sort of go out. Girls have such a different social dynamic, there's the popular girls or the non-popular girls, and you're trying to strive to be as good as you can, on top of academics and sports, and conditioning for the sports. Like I'm working out four times a week on top of my practices, with my mom and

my sisters, and then taking care of my sister because my parents are working. And then you're supposed to try on top of that to go hang out with your friends.

When asked if girls have male siblings and if the parental expectations of them are different, Alex, a vivacious U14 player, responded:

By far. They want him to make it to college. They want me to make it college, make it to med school, be a doctor, and play soccer and all these sports at the same time. And in order to do that, I have to keep my grades at an A in everything and do all this. It's not physically possible. Or mentally. I don't want to make the choice to drop something. I like everything. I like playing all my sports. I like doing everything. Obviously I have to make a change, but I don't want to. I have to.

Chelsea, who is just one year older, added more details regarding these burdens on teenage girls:

It's the pressure to be perfect. Because girls, something about our society, we have this standard to look up to, to be perfect at everything, good at sports, smart, pretty, nice, and popular, and it's just kind of annoying how we all have to be like that, or try to be.

Several girls mentioned how the pressures subsequently affected their physical health. Some spoke about falling asleep while doing homework, feeling cranky, not giving 100% to any one component of their lives, and feeling like a failure. Multi-sport athletes felt these strains the most. Geri, a teammate of Chelsea's, commented:

Sometimes I find it hard, and I think coaches sometimes need to understand a bit. With all the sports, like school sports, spring is hard with lacrosse. Some days we're going straight from lacrosse to soccer and I don't get home until 9. And I still have homework to do. And that's my problem. I'm taking these honor courses. I've been injuring and pulling muscles in my legs, and I've gone to trainers who tell me I'm overworking my body. And I really feel like coaches need to keep in mind like during the spring, there is spring sports like track and all that, *and* academics.

When I asked girls how they keep going, despite pressures, exhaustion, and performance demands, they seemed anxious. Alex, a U14 player, said:

I'm already told that I have to make a decision next year. I can't keep doing this. I can't stay up that late. I can't get up at 5:30 every morning and only get five and a half hours sleep. I need to make a change.

When I posited that girls their age need 10 hours of sleep a night, Alex's teammates added, "I'm so used to getting up at 5:40, I can't sleep in", and Erica described why lessening their load feels like a form of failure in itself:

Last year, I had so many activities I would wake up early in the morning and I wouldn't get home at all until 9 o'clock at night, I'd be out of the house from 7:30 or 8 in the morning and I wouldn't be home in that time at all… My mom and dad, they don't like me to quit things. Once the season or session is over, then I can choose to drop something, but not in the middle of it, and I understand that and agree with it, because I made a commitment and I have to stick with it. But it's exhausting after a really long time.

Yet it was Alex's comment that really left me feeling deeply troubled about parental expectations and desires for our children:

> I think my parents are the most supportive people. Because with everything I'm doing, it's hard to manage it all. As much as it sometimes seems like they're guilting you to do all that they want you to do, they care more than anyone, and that's the only reason they're so hard on me. It creates separation between you and your parents. It tends to be parents live their life through their child. And when this happens, they want everything that they did wrong to be right with their children. I've been told this by my mom. She says she wants me to be amazing at soccer because she never reached her full potential at soccer. It's like they want us to succeed as much as we want to succeed, and sometimes they push us the wrong way, and sometimes they push us too much. And it can create tension and anxiety between parents and children.

My research showed that girls faced a complex array of social and parental pressures. What is critical for coaches and administrators to understand is that the girls didn't leave those pressures on the field, but carried them into practices and games simultaneously. Thus, their private stressors became intertwined with their public performances.

I was left wondering how to address the inequities and private struggles that our female athletes were facing. The answer was

GO BEECHWOOD, (GO stands for girls and opportunities), a free additional program for the club's female players that focused on whole body wellness, (which I hoped would increase girls' self-awareness), advocacy skills and overall confidence as female athletes.

DESIGNING GO BEECHWOOD: A GIRLS' INITIATIVE

The GO BEECHWOOD program (GB)—with the tagline *Go farther, stronger, together*—evolved out of three main areas in the focus group findings: perceived inequities; lack of collective consciousness and solidarity; and the need for greater advocacy and recognition. It is important to note that these findings resonated with much of the aforementioned literature. The initiative speaks to Welford's (2011) desire for girls and women to have broader decision-making and leadership roles; to Caudwell's (2011) push for more research on situated experiences; and to Keathley's (2013) call to address team dynamics, pressures, and gender-focused knowledge. GB was therefore structured to have three components: (1) educational resources and tools, (2) integrative team-building and multi-age activities that speak to girls' desire for fun and high levels of enjoyment within soccer, and (3) a fun mentoring and leadership component that speaks to girls' critical emphasis on relational issues. The program brought in national speakers and local medical experts to discuss the mental aspect of the game, nutrition, concussions, ACL injury prevention and treatment, and how to prepare for and enter college soccer. In addition, the girls were given the opportunity to build peer relationships with other girls, as they spoke so highly of such relationships in the data. Working closely with the DOC, our hope was that GO BEECHWOOD would eventually be a space where girls could develop their voices and self-advocacy skills and become change-makers in their own lives.

As such, we crafted a mission statement that aligned itself closely with that of the club: *To provide our female Beechwood players with diverse learning opportunities that will increase their self-awareness, advocacy skills, and overall confidence as female athletes.* We also wrote a specific vision and value statement: *GO BEECHWOOD is a program of excellence that focuses on the whole-body wellness of female athletes and as such the program includes social and psychological development and training, exposure to educational resources and experts, and becoming a positive role model and peer pal, all while creating memorable, life experiences among Beechwood girls.*

The GB program, which is still running today, is not designed to solve all the issues that these girls are facing, but rather is a response to the concerns raised in the focus groups about their experiences in a male-dominated environment. As such, I believe the GB model can be used in many other soccer clubs and sport environments to enrich the experiences of female athletes. I address specifically how this might be done in the final chapter within this book.

CONCLUSIONS

My research shows that girls want to be equal to their male counterparts in many ways. They have as much of a competitive spirit, but often feel coaches coddle them or treat them differently just because of their gender. They want to be pushed and challenged, and yet also face internal struggles to be perfect. Such complex scenarios find girls struggling to be seen as equal talent-wise at practice or on the field with their male counterparts, while struggling internally to be perfect not only as athletes, but as students, daughters, and friends off the field. Such a dichotomy of gendered expectations points to the fact that until soccer clubs document girls' specific experiences, they will not know why girls are leaving or how to better retain them on their rosters. More research needs to be done with girls in urban areas—and in broader global contexts—to see if these same struggles exist there. My research on game face and girl face, however, adds rich, new data that allow us to better understand girls within male-dominated clubs at present. Such research is critical in today's quickly growing youth soccer environment.

Chapter 3

The Athena Complex:
Female Soccer Players and Their
Hyper-Invested Parents

I strode across the parking lot on a crisp fall morning, in a leafy, bucolic New England town of New Malden[13]. I eyed the rec park fields at a distance, amazed at the massive number of little kids moving in circles like bees in a beehive; their tiny cleats scraping the soggy ground, searching for the elusive ball. What struck me was not just the large number of tiny little soccer players, but the fact that many of the coaches were women. It soon became apparent that it wasn't just that they were women—they were soccer moms. Arriving newcomers seemed unsure what field they were playing on, given that there were no numbers and no identifiers. "Oh, Ella, you're on Argentina with Sophie's mom, she's over there. See there (pointing toward the trees lining the riverbank)? With the yellow sweatshirt and Celtics hat?" Similar conversations played out over and over in a short amount of time

---

13   All names of locations, people, and organizations in this chapter have been changed to protect confidentiality.

that morning. Girls and boys all under the age of 7 were there to learn the beautiful game of soccer, and it appeared that parents, particularly moms, were going to help them learn the sport.

A few days later, Virginia, a mom of three daughters in a town only 20 minutes from New Malden, recounted to me how her girls, too, wanted to join their local recreation team, but she had inadvertently missed the deadline. When she called the local rec team organizer, she was told, "Well, actually we don't have enough coaches, so if you want to have your daughters play, you are going to have to sign up to be the coach!" Virginia felt so guilty she agreed, even though she had never played soccer, let alone taught others how to do the same. Thankfully her husband asked two of his junior colleagues (both former soccer players) to help out. The two of them graciously showed up for weekly practice as well as the Saturday games to help his wife out. It ended up being a winning equation for all involved.

One evening, later that same fall, I ventured into the local indoor center of a dynamic soccer club nearby in Beechwood (hereafter called BSC for Beechwood Soccer Club). The building was housed in a vast complex, with numerous industrial-looking buildings. The soccer facility—replete with indoor turf, multiple goals, and netting to separate various fields—had a row of chairs on one side for spectator parents. Banners hung proudly on the wall directly across from the parent viewing area, designating sponsoring businesses that ranged from hair salons and construction firms to churches and insurance companies. What was most unusual in this venue however was not the setting, but the fact that at the practices that evening (for girls aged 10-14), there was not one female coach or mother on the fields anywhere (except myself who was there to collect data). There were men—several quite young-looking—all striding around in black track pants and sweatshirts emblazoned with various sports emblems. They moved swiftly, circling in and out of the players, announcing the drills and patterns they wanted deftly executed. The players listened intently and focused on the matter at hand. Additionally, as I looked around the parent viewing area, the sparsely filled seats were taken up predominantly by males (dads, more specifically, as I heard them yelling at their daughters). One man yelled out to his daughter, "You've got this Kar, don't let her get by you!" Why was it that so few women were involved in coaching or even spectating among these older girls? Why were there only fathers overseeing the practices, which in turn were dominated by male coaches? This chapter addresses that interesting and complex dynamic in youth soccer: the role that modern parents—particularly fathers—play in shaping the lives of their modern soccer-playing athlete daughters. I call this complicated relationship the Athena complex, harkening back to the Greek mythological story of Athena, who was Zeus' favorite, and most trusted, daughter (Hamilton, p. 25). She was literally born out of Zeus' head, and, as such, was a talented, clever, strong warrior. Thus, she was often an agent, as Wilson (2007) puts it, for Zeus' commands. Yet, her story of affection and ability is not without turmoil; Synodinou (1986) notes that Athena was afraid of upsetting her father and often suppressed her true feelings (pp. 160–161).

My findings show that the daughters within this one club had parents who wanted the very best for their capable daughters, but who didn't always know where to draw the line of intrusion and overprotectiveness. I often focus on the fathers in this chapter, not because their actions were worse than the mothers, but because they often get left out of the analysis about females and soccer.

Today there is a cultural expectation and acceptance for mothers to support and cheer on their daughters' advancement and successes in society (which is clearly laudable and important). Yet, I argue here that such a normative model ignores the crucial role that fathers play in their daughters' social and athletic development arc. I believe that more research needs to be done on fathers in particular; that, in turn, relates to my findings in chapter 6 about gender-aware men and their roles in helping further women's causes in athletics. If we don't add men into our analysis of women's lives, males become outliers and absent in the broader gender discourse.

Within the Beechwood soccer environment, it was the dads that were often the ones who first got their daughters into soccer, and encouraged them to stay. Yet, what do we know about how the female athletes feel about their dad's roles? My research answers that question by showing that these fathers (rightly) yearn for positive success for their clever, articulate, bright, driven, talented daughters, but the problem lies in how some of them try to help their daughters reach that end point.

FINDINGS

My data reveals that parents exerted two types of gendered control strategies: (1) open, overt messages (what I label as resolute verbal control which was used by both mothers and fathers) toward their daughters' playing ability; and (2) non-communicative behavior approaches such as silent treatment responses, socio-emotional pressures that were hidden and covert, and layers of masked structural control (most often employed by fathers). In some ways, I knew that the verbal control would exist, as I had witnessed it during my research period at BSC, but what was most intriguing and troubling was the non-communicative and structural control approaches by fathers that I had not witnessed, given their hidden, concealed nature.

It should be noted that neither approach felt better than the other to the girls and young women involved; each strategy felt difficult in its respective, situated context[14]. In saying that, I should add that the athletes also felt very cognizant (and conflicted) that their parents, and fathers particularly, knew a great deal about soccer (several of them were former high school and collegiate athletes) and that in addition both parents had sacrificed a large amount of time and money to involve their daughters in this magical sport. The players criticized the barrage of negative information and comments from fathers and yet often simultaneously touted it as okay, given the pivotal roles their fathers played in their early developmental years as their first coaches. The girls and young women seem to reframe their fathers' negative comments or, in some cases, simply minimize them. Such complex feelings are evidence that daughters do not respond to or understand fathering (or parenting in general) in simple, absolute ways, and often experience emotional dissonance about such behaviors and information.

It is important to note that fathers and mothers most likely did not intend for these actions to be hurtful, but unfortunately at times that was in fact the resulting impact. What is most important in my findings is not what the parents' intentions were, but how their behavior strategies actually impacted their daughters' sense of

---

14 One U14 girl, Maureen, summed up how hard all parental pressure was: "I hate when my parents talk to me about soccer. Because they always have something bad to say."

self. I must note that as I did not study the parents themselves, I believe that more research needs to be focused on these individuals, particularly the fathers, in order to fully understand these complex feminist father/daughter relationships.

THE PUBLIC MESSAGES: RESOLUTE VERBAL CONTROL

Many girls talked initially in our focus groups about the overt expressions of pressure by both of their parents. One U14 player said, "The parents are always on the sideline and they're yelling at us." Alex added, "My mom doesn't understand what I'm doing, like I'm waiting for a pass and she's like, 'Why aren't you running?'" Her teammate added, "They're not the ones actually out there playing," and "they don't understand the game like we do. And they think they understand, but they just don't."

Parents who engaged in such verbal outbursts were doing so to help their daughters become better athletes, but the daughters felt embarrassed and frustrated by such public displays of emotion and critique. Elizabeth, a U13 player, recounted her angst over the outbursts and even explained her attempts to curb them:

> My parents, my dad, he's very into my soccer and he's very demanding about it. And so both of my parents will be on the sideline and I'm sure all you guys hear them yelling at me, "Elizabeth push harder, come on, that girl just beat you, you should be better than that!" I remember when I was younger—because I don't play those positions any more—but I used to always play the outside and I'd never want to be on the side of the

field my parents were on, because they'd yell at me like crazy. And I've talked to my parents and said, "I feel like when you're yelling and screaming at me on the field, that's not supporting me."

Later she added that her parent's response to her was, "We'll try to do this, but we're just trying to encourage you," and her response was "I understand that and I appreciate your efforts, but it's not working for what I'm doing." She shook her head with disgust, letting out an extended sigh, as she finished her commentary.

Other girls shared similar stories of critical parents, but one teammate, Krista, went deeper in her analysis, noting that harsh criticism might be more helpful if her parents actually knew more about the sport that they were commenting on. Krista felt that the overt comments were often hollow and unfounded:

> Well, personally, I just wish that my parents—they've gotten into our sports, one of my brothers and me, he's really athletic and I'm relatively athletic, like we both ski and play soccer, and now lacrosse. And sometimes I feel like it would make me a better player, not if my parents hounded me about what I did wrong, but if they, instead of just driving us to practice and paying the bills to be part of clubs like this, maybe took the time to read some things about skills and how to help and stuff like that. So that when they watch a game, they can really help me pinpoint what I've done wrong because a lot of times, it's me searching for what I've done wrong and what I can do better, that makes me psych myself out and puts me in a terrible mood as a player. But if I could

have that support from my parents, not in the form of harsh, critical observations, but in the form of help.

Mary, a young U12 player, echoed Krista's comments, specifically describing how her dad expected the most, even when she had little to give, due to her exhaustion. Mary felt that her mother was much more lenient about effort and ability, while her dad never wanted her to let up. The girls felt this overt pressure to be stifling and difficult to put up with:

> I was talking to my mom about it actually and she said sometimes boys don't understand that, how to give good feedback. Because I felt like my dad was putting pressure on me. I was practicing and I got up late that day, and I was really tired, and I was really stressed out, and I had to hurry, hurry, hurry that day before practice, and by the time practice came around, I didn't have anything left to give. I had something for school practice, but then after goalie practice, he goes, "Mary, you need to give more and give your best," and I was giving my best, but my best wasn't anything. We got into this big argument about how he needed to be a little bit more understanding and stuff. And I kept telling him, "That's why Mom goes to practice!" Because my mom is just more like, she gives me, "You can do better," but she's like quick about it. She doesn't dwell on it, and be like, "You need to do that!" But you know like you have nothing and then blah, blah, blah. That's what my dad does, but Mom just goes, "You need to be quicker on the ball and I know you're working on that, so good job working on it."

Such criticism took a toll on these girls. Margaret, a U14 girl, said this:

> I think what my parents don't realize is, they're trying to help me and give me advice so I can become a better player, but they don't realize that their criticism just makes you feel miserable about yourself and sometimes you don't want to do it anymore, because you don't feel like you're getting any improvement, because they keep going like, "Oh, you could do this better, you're not getting any better," and you just want to quit.

The women's feelings regarding parental expectations were multilayered and complicated. Many of the respondents valued that their fathers had played soccer, or at least had been collegiate athletes, and thus the girls felt such backgrounds gave fathers a "right" to comment, but it was often the timing of the delivery that wasn't always helpful.

A U14 player summed up the difficulties surrounding the daughter/dad relationship:

> My dad was a coach at Beechwood so he knows a lot about soccer, but I think they could just get better about how they tell me stuff. After you play a bad game, that's the last thing you want to hear—that it's okay to mess up.

A different player, who was on the U16 team, stated

> Well for me, my dad grew up ski racing and playing soccer, and I'm a ski racer and a soccer player and so

in skiing he instructs me and helps me, but sometimes it makes me upset. But in soccer, I feel like there isn't pressure, it's just constructive criticism, because I'm sure my dad was a good soccer player, so he knows what to say I guess. But it's not bad pressure, it's helpful. It's just after games, he'll tell me what he thinks I did badly.

The girls felt that such knowledge was valuable, yet often they felt it came with obligations and expectations. They felt that their moms and dads had given so much to them, both financially and in terms of time. A U14 player voiced:

And my dad is really into soccer…he coached me…He's really into it and he loves it, and both my parents played it when they were younger. But they know that they were never as good as my sister and I are, because they didn't have the coaches that we have and stuff. And they really support us. But at the same time, they know our full potential, so if we're having an off game, they'll compare it to a better game. And at times, it's like, I can't play like that all the time. Everyone has a bad game, everyone has a bad day. And I've tried telling my parents, "Just lay off, okay? I tried the best I could and, I'm sorry, I wasn't feeling well that day." But then they'll get upset because they'll think you're being ungrateful about all the money and time they're putting into this.

The athletes also felt torn that their dads had brought them up in this sport, yet also simultaneously put unspoken pressures upon them. Such a conundrum left them feeling flummoxed; they often rationalized that such pressures were difficult, yet in turn valuable. Another U14 player said this:

My dad's been my soccer coach for a really long time. So for school he's been my soccer coach ever since I was really little, like 2nd or 3rd grade. So in switching over to Beechwood, I feel like he's taught me a lot, and he has high expectations. He puts a lot of pressure on me to do everything that I've learned, I guess.

Erica had a very similar comment:

The reason that I was started in soccer is because of my dad, because he played soccer and that was the reason that I was signed up in the beginning. When I was little, I went to all the little soccer camps because he wanted me to, but I love soccer.

Irina, a U13 player, spoke to the fact that because her father had been a coach, he felt that he could judge her soccer ability much more keenly. Ironically, this led to the same sort of resolute verbal control (open overt messages) that Elizabeth's dad exerted:

My dad pressures me a whole lot, because he used to be a coach. Yeah, it's really bad. Basically, after every game, they focus more on what I did wrong than what I did well. Because I was pretty much the only person who cared about soccer in Dallas and so it was just really hard with them constantly nagging me about it. I like to hear tips and stuff on how I can improve, but they were really getting on me about it and it got to the point where I was just sort of over it. When we came here, I played my first school soccer game and nobody was yelling. Everybody on the sidelines was yelling nothing, except for my parents. And it was so embarrassing, because you hear your dad and your mom yelling things at you, so everyone knows it's your parents. It's really embarrassing.

Sue lamented about her dad's running commentary despite never being a soccer player (see previous comments from Sue in chapter 2 under the Girl Face section):

And obviously in practice, I'm going to mess up, it's not like I'm on a professional team or anything. I'm just in practice, but it's always screaming how to do everything even though he's never played soccer in his life. And then he starts yelling at other people, but that's a whole other story.

This research shows that girls yearned to feel encouraged, heard, and actually buoyed up by their parents, in what they called a helpful way. To the girls and young women, the unfounded comments or analysis of the game were not valuable, constructive, or authentic. It turns out that such parental input is more common than we realize. Steve Henson (2012) comments on the survey data of Brown and Miller which shows that kids' worst memory from youth sports was the ride home from games with their parents. Henson restates their findings that show "before the sweat has even dried on the child's uniform," (p. 2) parents often jump right in and start commenting on what went wrong or what didn't. Similarly, the female athletes I met wanted parents who supported them, who were not always harping on their failings and wrongdoings, yet they also valued their parent's knowledge when it came from a place of experience. It was experience that often shaped the dads' views, as many of them had coached in the past, and thus felt very comfortable in this soccer world. Such familiarity, though, bred an environment where they felt they were in control, could take control, and always knew what was best for their daughters, even if the daughters felt differently.

THE PRIVATE MESSAGES: MASKED CONTROL AND SILENCE

The other type of strategy that fathers used to control their daughters' soccer experiences was varying forms of uncommunicative social behavior. The most common form of taciturn regulation by fathers was what girls referred to as the silent treatment. This strategy was often employed after a game in which a daughter was perceived as not having played well. The fathers would then not speak to them at all during the inevitable long car ride home. As I mentioned in the previous chapter, Georgia, a U15 player, often feels like she is letting her dad down due to his own sports enthusiasm and expectations:

> I can't live up to his expectations and when that happens, I feel like I'm letting him down. And then I just sort of get down on myself. ….. And sometimes it's a silent pressure. Like after a really bad game, like in the car he won't just say, good job, or tell me what I did wrong, he'll just be silent the entire way home so during that time, you just overanalyze what's gone on in the game and you feel like it's the worst game of your life, even though it might not have been.

These unique forms of pressure were nonverbal in nature and yet the girls and young women knew exactly what the real message was. One U15 player said this about her dad:

My parents, in particular my dad, he's the soccer parent, and he puts a lot of pressure on me because he's been with me through the experiences at different clubs. And he likes all the parents here and he likes the coaches, so he expects me to do a lot better, because there's better people and players and coaches. And some of the pressure he puts on me, I double with my own pressure I put on myself. And I feel the more he pressures me, like I want to do better, but it also starts to freak me out to the point where I can't handle it and I don't know how to play. I get so into my mind where I don't know what to do.

Other high school players noted that their parents weren't talking to them directly, but were talking about them, or to others behind their backs. One U15 player recounted this feeling that also created a non-verbalized pressure or intensity:

A lot of times, they'll underestimate me and that kind of makes me underestimate myself, because sometimes having no pressure makes me feel they don't understand how big a part of my life this is, and sometimes it makes me feel like I can't do things. Like when school soccer season rolled around, sometimes I would hear my parents having conversations like how they didn't think I would make a certain team, and that would kind of make me undermine myself, when I really shouldn't do that.

Ironically though, girls felt that they added their own internal pressures when parents were too over-supportive. Her teammate said this:

I'd struggle with that a lot and put pressure on myself, because I'd think that I needed to improve in one area, when I really didn't need to improve in that area and I feel like it was also, at least in my family, it was pressure/no pressure from my parents, because they'd say, "Oh it's okay, you did your best," all the time instead of giving me some criticism, and I feel like it was pressure/no pressure because the pressure came from myself and when my parents kept telling me there was absolutely no pressure, it only increased my want to be better and the pressure I put on myself.

Another U15 player added:

After a practice, she'll say, "You did really well, but you passed back during a scrimmage and it was bad," and I'll say, "It's really not like that."

One U14 player summed it up this way:

I think that there's different types of pressure. There's pressure that makes you want to be better and motivates you, and there's pressure that just tears you down. Like if someone was to say, "You had a really bad game," it really gets to you, I guess. And if someone on the field says something to you, it's sort of something you can use to get better, I guess.

Another young player noted that at a team meeting near tryout times, she remembered that even other players' parents were criticizing her openly about playing multiple sports! They stated they weren't sure she was a full-team player. She recounted:

I think, I'm not gonna list names or whatever, they said I couldn't play on the A team because I wasn't committed enough. And I didn't make the goalie practices, so I had no right to play goalie. Which just made me very pressured. (See definition for A team qualifications in footnote within chapter 2)

Ironically, and very painfully, in this instance, her father said nothing. When I asked her why that was, she replied, "Yeah, and my dad just stayed silent because obviously, there was no reason to fight."

Another arena where fathers engaged in nonverbal pressure was collegiate expectations. Several older girls (16 and 17 at the time of the focus groups) spoke about the dilemma of dads who expected them to play collegiate athletics, when they weren't even sure they wanted to continue playing high school soccer. This angst over having a difficult conversation was compounded by the fact that the girls felt that they owed their parents for the countless hours and large sums of money that the parents, particularly dads, had invested in this club sport activity. Audrey and Jane both worried about their respective parents' expectations, given their intense financial and time commitment (see prior quotes from these athletes in chapter 2 under the Girl Face section).

One of Audrey's teammates echoed similar comments, noting that her own parents pressured her to attend ID college camps, despite her resistance. In many ways, all of these girls spoke similarly about trying to balance their lives with multiple activities.

That's what Audrey said, about not knowing. I've gotten these emails for all these camps during the summer. And

I don't know if I want to go, because I don't know if I want to play. But then I don't want to not go if I end up wanting to play. It's like just balancing. Because I know I'd be doing a lot of other stuff during the summer and I'd be missing two or three weeks. Like social stuff, definitely summer's a huge social and I'd be missing all that.

One other way that fathers used masked control was by fraternizing with the coaches. This strategy seemed innocuous enough to outsiders, but the girls were smart enough to see beyond and through it. Such bonding and relationships made the girls feel uncomfortable and again showed the fathers' dominance in structuring and determining the boundaries and relationships surrounding their daughters' soccer experience. Alex, a U14 player, said this about her coach and her own dad:

After the game, he was saying things like, "Good playing, nice ball." And he said some short things, but then later I found, when we went to bed, my dad went down to the bar with Jeff and him. So my dad knows more about him than I do.

Having her dad socialize with the coach made her feel uncomfortable and somewhat awkward. It left her feeling that she was the outsider, when in fact, she was supposed to be the one advocating for herself. Audrey, the U16 player, echoed such imbalance:

This goes back to the skills thing. I just remember when I played for Thunder, I was with my dad and he was talking to the director Thunder person. He was like "Oh

yeah, Audrey's good but she just doesn't have the same
skills the boys do, because she doesn't get to practice
with them, she has to practice with the girls and she
doesn't get that same level."

Audrey felt that her dad was the one telling the coach what to do,
and she was left out of the equation. Girls were then left feeling
like their voices weren't the ones that mattered in the sport, but
their dads' voices made a difference. Ironically, the dads probably
felt that they were just helping, but couldn't see how it made their
daughters feel—worthless and invisible.

CONCLUSIONS

My research shows that despite their best intentions, fathers
(and mothers) are affecting their own daughters' experiences
in youth soccer. These female athletes—as do all young girls
and women—just want to be truly seen, heard, and validated.
Unfortunately, their fathers' own views of sport, soccer, and
what they believe will help their daughters in the future obscured
their ability to see or hear what their daughters really wanted in
this environment. Such miscommunication and lack of difficult
conversations negatively impacted how the girls experienced
soccer. In the focus groups, I had girls openly weep and share
how hard these multi-layered pressures are. When asked "How
many of you have ever had a moment where you've said, 'I don't
think I want to do this anymore' because of the criticisms?" every
single person raised a hand. Chelsea, a U15 player, said, "They
want me playing above the level so that I'm getting better. And
sometimes I think they don't hear me. Like I want to play above
the level, but sometimes they push it so much that I don't want

to play anymore." Such comments echo the distress felt by Erica, the U14 player described in chapter 2 who wanted to quit (under the Girl Face section), but was compelled by her parents to stay until the end. She felt she had no choice, other than to stay and feel exhausted.

The findings in this research are a wake-up call for fathers and mothers, everywhere. If they keep pressuring daughters in this manner, these female athletes might feel compelled to lash out, like Athena, or worse, choose to give up on the beautiful sport that has given them so many social, emotional, and physical benefits.

Chapter 4

Looking for the Trophy, Not the Fight: How Gender Microaggressions Diminish the Experience of Collegiate Division II and III Athletes

---

*The greatest feeling in the world is when you're on the
field and you know that your team is going
to succeed because you look around and see your ten
best friends playing beside you.*

—quote from a Division III locker room whiteboard, 2016

In this chapter, I focus on 24 collegiate athletes (14 from a D2 team and 10 from a D3 team) from two leafy campuses, in the same busy soccer conference north of the Mason-Dixon line. In some ways these two teams were quite different. The D3 team represented a small university that was rural and isolated in terms of its location; had recently experienced an undefeated soccer season; and was comprised of athletes that exuded a remarkable, almost palpable, family-type bond and chemistry (highlighted in the locker room quote above). In contrast, the D2 team, situated near a major city, had a more complicated team chemistry, with more age-group cliques as opposed to entire team bonding; had barely won any games in the prior season; and spoke strongly and openly about their frustrations and defeats. All in all, these teams could not be any more different from each other, yet what the data revealed was that all of the women spoke vehemently— and almost identically—about the wider student body perceptions of them, and their overall experiences of being female collegiate athletes.

It turns out that campus location, coach's gender, or vastly different conference records did not reveal major differences in how they were perceived by others both on and off campus. What turns out to be most significant for these respondents is that people saw them first as a female, and only later as athletes. These collegiate players found it frustrating—and, from their points of view, downright insulting—that "athlete" was an addendum and "woman" was the primary identifier.

These women did not want to be called a female athlete. West and Zimmerman (2009) call these adjectives "special qualifiers, such as 'female doctor' or 'male nurse' that must be added to exceptions to the rule" (p. 129). The collegiate women I met wanted to be seen not as exceptions, but just as athletes (who happen to be women). As such, in this chapter, and hereafter, I use the term *f/athlete* to reflect their desire to be seen as athletes without deeper gender analysis and attachments while still referring to the broader sociological understanding that gender does indeed matter. My findings show that gender *does* significantly shape athlete experiences in their respective environments, but not always in ways that they want it to. The women wanted to be seen as powerful, strong, and competitive student-athletes. Full stop. Unfortunately, what they encountered were student bodies (on two radically different campuses) that conceptualized gender as their most important signifying variable (before athleticism), not the other way around as these athletes had hoped[15].

These women believed strongly that athletics, strength, and ability were enough and that the gender label shouldn't matter to a great extent. Such findings resonate clearly with the work of Martin and Phillips (2017) who show that gender blindness in male- dominated environments is a strategy that women use to downplay gender in order to increase female confidence (p. 28). I believe that such narratives are tied to the same narratives that we see with the younger middle school and high school girls (see chapter 2). These young women have all been raised to believe they can do anything and be anything, yet in reality once they enter into male-dominated environs, the starkness and intensity of sexism and discrimination is hard to avoid. Revealing these women's desires for gender indifference in 2019 is critical to a complete picture of gender and sport. We must expose and deconstruct the paradoxes and complexities of women's identities as athletes to better see their full female selves. As Michael Ian Black put it in his February 21, 2018 NYT article:

> The past 50 years have redefined what it means to be
> female in America. Girls today are told that they can do

---

15   In her 2013 book *Lean In* Sheryl Sandberg wonders what it would be like "to go
      through life without being labeled by my gender" (134). These athletes wanted
      the same. Sandberg argues that "the subject itself presents a paradox, forcing us
      to acknowledge differences while trying to achieve the goal of being treated the
      same."

anything, be anyone. They've absorbed the message: They're outperforming boys in school at every level. But it isn't just about performance. To be a girl today is to be the beneficiary of decades of conversation about the complexities of womanhood, its many forms and expressions. (Black, 2018)

My research on younger athletes and collegiate athletes shows that while women have absorbed the feminist "be all" message, they now do not understand why the rest of the world hasn't come alongside such belief systems.

Moreover, my work shows that these collegiate athletes experienced gender microaggressions, particularly microinsults and microinvalidations. Sue et al (2007) point out that racial microaggressions are "brief and commonplace daily verbal, behavioral, and environmental indignities, whether intentional or unintentional, that communicate hostile, derogatory, or negative racial slights and insults to the target person or group" (p. 273). Using this crucial historical piece, coupled with the more recent work of Basford, Offermann, and Behrend (2014), I apply this microaggression framework to gender environments within soccer. Basford and her colleagues note that gender microaggressions are "intentional or unintentional actions or behaviors that exclude, demean, insult, oppress, or otherwise express hostility or indifference toward women" (p. 341). I found f/athletes faced gender microinsults through being seen as sexualized objects or by the belief that female players are second-class citizens, as well as through microinvalidations by which their experiences were nullified and thus they became invisible, resulting in what Sue refers to as feeling like "an alien in [one's] own land" (p. 278).

In this chapter, I outline three gender microaggression themes that emerged from the data for these f/athletes: being labeled as other, being seen as sexualized objects, and positive and negative marked identities on campus. Finally I detail their response to such invalidations, which was to build and exhibit a strong familial-type bond.

Labeled as Other	• Girls' sports not valued • Few fans • Thought of as less talented
Sexualized Objects	• Males watch to see bodies, not skill • Slut shaming on social media
Marked Campus Identities	• Positive: Identity as "on a team" on campus • Negative: Given fewer resources
Team Bond	• Sense of family

I should note here before I deconstruct my findings that, just like their younger female counterparts, these players wanted to talk about their experiences. As one f/athlete put it, "You should come more often," with another adding, "That would be sweet. You're hired!" Others spoke in agreement about how important it is to hear women's voices, and yet in most cases, as I mentioned earlier, it is rare—with one athlete calling it a "nice unfiltered talk"—that their input is valued or even heard[16]. One D2 player put it most succinctly in terms of how sharing these views was often not available to them:

---

16 In this chapter, I don't name the collegiate players individually as they often spoke over one another, making the transcription details hard to separate by athlete. Instead, I choose to designate them by their respective schools. I will use D2 for a Division II athlete and D3 for the Division III athletes.

We're not as recognized as often—female athletes, I guess—and when we're kind of focused on and pinpointed, that's when we feel more comfortable to voice what we're really feeling and how we're seen around campus. So when we get to talk about it to you, it's also really signaling some feelings you can release comfortably and be able to voice I guess, in a more natural, casual setting. It's better than talking to coach, I guess, when you have to be more professional and more normal, and kind of gotta watch what you say a little bit, sometimes. And you aren't always able to say what you like and what you don't like.

I specifically remember that, toward the end of the D3 focus group, I told them that we had about a half an hour left, and a player blurted, "OH NO!" When I asked her why that was her response she said, "I'm having fun! It's nice to get everything out and talk." A teammate added, "I just said to Tracy in the bathroom that I like to have my voice heard because I feel like we don't get to talk about this enough. Nobody asks." Another stated, "Nobody asks us how we feel, why we are important. It's just a nice feeling." Such comments illustrate how few opportunities there are for female players to have their voices heard and, subsequently, how rare such qualitative data collection is within the field of gender and sport.

RESEARCH PROCESS

Between April 2016 and January 2017, I obtained permission from the coaches and athletic directors, accepted signed consent forms from players, and interviewed the 24 athletes on their respective campuses. The interviews were typically held in small focus groups of 8-10 players and held in athletic building conference rooms. The interviews typically lasted for 2 hours, with the groups taking a small break in the middle. In each focus group, the interviews were taped, and later transcribed and typed up for future use.

The first school I arrived at—to interview the D3 team—was in a rural location with little traffic and a peaceful ambience. It was clear that the campus buildings were newer than the town and that the school had put a lot of money into infrastructure. Upon entering the lobby of the athletic center where the focus group would be held, I noticed typical athletic building décor— the school name and mascot adorned the walls in large, colorful motifs. In addition, trophy cases lined the walls, with multiple awards and trophies from conference wins. Finally, large wooden banners decorated the walls noting various NCAA appearances and conference championship wins; I counted 100 recognized team appearances since 1985.

Similar décor was found at the institution with the D2 team. The school—set near a large, busy city—was similarly well manicured with beautiful tree-lined walkways. Their athletic center also housed trophy cases and banners documenting NCAA wins and appearances. The walls of the lobby were embellished with larger-than-life pictures of female and male athletes in each varsity sport. Such inviting images became familiar adornments every time I walked into a new athletic center to interview a team or a head coach.

Yet no matter what type of campus I arrived at, the sociological findings were the same. The f/athletes were conceptualized as lesser—or "other"—in comparison to their male counterparts;

were viewed as sexualized objects; and had a marked identity (both positive and negative) on campus; and yet the teams had strong, familial-type bonds.

FEMALE SPORTS AS "OTHER": JUST A GIRL'S GAME

These collegiate players feel identified as different by other students on campus, male soccer players, and, at times (for the D2 players), even by their coach. They don't want to be seen in this unique, gendered light, but they experience people treating them in unique ways simply because they are women.

The players, first and foremost, noted in our focus groups that they were never seen as fully able as their male soccer counterparts on campus. Being a female athlete meant being less valued and less worthy in comparison to male athletes. Even when the team had a female coach, as the D2 team did, their same-gender relationship was complicated; they wanted her to be tougher, more direct, and less emotive.

A recurrent theme of the f/athletes was feeling undervalued and invisible. The D3 players I met were particularly saddened that in their college, despite their incredible fall season (which occurred just before I interviewed them), they got little recognition from non-soccer players and even less recognition from non-athletes. One D3 player put it this way:

> I feel like a lot of the time too, if we win or we played a hard game, I've heard guys be like, "Well, it's a girls' sport, so why does it even matter?" And I'm like,

"We just worked for 90 minutes, just like you did."
Or we won the [conference] and the boys didn't. And
it comes down to when we play, I find that we don't
have as many fans, but when the guys play, it's like the
stadium's full and it's annoying really. We work just as
hard and we do everything the guys do, but we don't get
the same recognition for it.

When asked why they thought this was true, they noted that fans
want to see the boys play as their style of play is more interesting.
One D3 player noted, "I think people assume that since we're girls,
it's not gonna be a good game, maybe." When I prodded, "What does
a 'good game' mean in that sentence?" They all jumped in, "Fast.
Upbeat. Aggressive. Fancy moves. Physical. For entertainment.
Everyone wants aggressiveness." But it was her teammate that
really deconstructed what the other players were thinking:

Everyone loves a good tackle. When you hear the slap up
in the stands. We get that. But they don't think we will
because we're girls, we're fragile. No, we're not. Girls are
more aggressive. We don't flop on the ground when we
get our toes stepped on and call for a red card. No, we get
back up. We've had girls that get their eye cut open, get
stitches, and come back. We have girls that have played
through so many injuries, and then you have the guys who
have a broken toe or a blister, and they're like, "I'm out
for the season." And it's like, what? That doesn't make
any sense. And yet we still don't get the recognition.

Another D3 teammate jumped into the conversation, adding
how frustrating it is to be constantly compared to her male
counterparts:

I feel that we're not respected as a team like a men's team would be respected. It's important, knowing that I have 20-something girls around me that will always support me and always be my family, but other people don't care about that. We're still just women athletes, we're not going to get the same respect out there. People are like—the amount of times I've heard—throughout my entire career, my girls' high school team was way better than the boys' team. The boys' team was awful and people would be like, "Well they're boys, of course they beat you." People have said it here. We're a great team, we work hard, we're smart. And people are like, "The boys team could beat you, they'd blow you guys out of the water." And that's frustrating.

These comments point to the reality that women's sports are deemed different and deviant within a normative male framework within sports.

Another persistent theme in the collegiate focus groups was frustration at the popular belief (shared by their younger counterparts in chapter 2) that female athletes need to be coddled, guided, and treated differently due to their gender identity. As I showed in chapter 2, what they really want is caring, honest, and helpful criticism. The collegiate f/athletes were no different in this respect. One D2 player stated:

At least if a coach were to tell me, "You played 10%," that would make me want to work harder. At this level, I feel like I should be told "Listen, I'm sorry you sucked today, but you need to do something about it." And I would go in and do it.

Her teammate agreed:

> Like sometimes I wish I *was* told I sucked. There are
> times afterwards—everyone here can attest to this. We
> lost a couple of games—one game I whiffed the ball in
> the goal and we lost because of that. But I come off the
> field—and this happened like two games in a row—
> and they're [coaches] like, "It'll be better next time."
> It got to a point where I just wanted to be told that I
> sucked.

They lamented that, with their lousy record, being told "just
do better" wasn't helping them succeed. They wanted more,
and as one D2 f/athlete put it, they wanted to be told *how* to
become better. Such narratives speak to the complexity of
women being treated more gently because of their gender,
and the need for greater analysis of our gendered messages
in everyday conversation. Ironically, I assumed that the
f/athletes would always prefer a female coach who understood
what it meant to be a woman. However, in the case of these
D2 athletes, that was not always true in every situation. In
fact, the D2 players spoke passionately about how having
a female coach might be detrimental to their overall player
development. One D2 player said:

> I just think, personally—because I've had male coaches
> before—I think it's just that women are more sensitive,
> so when I had my club coach, who was a male, it was
> more direct, like he would tell you what he wanted
> you to do, and you'd do it. There's really no feelings
> involved or anything so that's why I think it's like
> different between male and female.

Her teammate added:

> I feel like for a male coach, it's very objective. Like, you played really poorly, this is what you need to do to improve. But a female coach, she'll be like, "If I say this, it might really hurt their feelings." They're more perceptive to how a female would react than a male coach might be.

I responded, "And you don't like that? Because I would want that. I would want someone to be perceptive to my feelings." One D2 woman replied "I want someone to just be honest with me. Like, 'Look, you played terribly today and this is what you need to do to improve,' instead of someone sugarcoating it and being like, 'Oh no, you kind of did all right. Here's a high five.'" Her teammates agreed that they often felt they didn't deserve high fives, and in fact, being offered a high five made them feel babied. One D2 woman said

> It's kind of insulting at some points, when you're like, "Okay, you did well, good job." But you're taking me off, and that doesn't make sense now. Like you look at me, and I look back at you, and we know. No words need to be exchanged, I know why I'm coming off.

They recounted the differences with male coaches, which seemed to focus on communication style and tone. Several respondents noted that male coaches were more direct, less emotive, and therefore more effective in helping them determine what to fix on the field. One D2 player mentioned:

> I know some club teams that I've been on, when it's a male coach, there is no emotional aspect of it. You don't worry about them asking you how you felt about that

game or anything. If you had a bad game, they'd be like, "You did this and this." And with [our coach] or any coach, I know after one game, she gave me a book about mind set and was like, "Read this book." And I was just like, "I'm reading a book?" Just a lot of stuff that you don't expect. I feel like a sport is what everyone wants to come to in order to forget about all the emotions or feelings except for the passion for the game. And she adds a lot of outside factors like, "How was your day? Did that impact your game?" And I was like, "No, I just had a bad game." Whereas as male coaches, they're just like "Why'd you have a bad game? You did this wrong." And that's what I kind of like about being on a team with a male coach.

There was acknowledgement among the collegiate athletes that men coach differently—and not always positively—but the difference is that the f/athletes see male coaches getting results. These f/athletes saw something within that coaching framework that appealed to their competitive natures. Her D2 teammate added:

To compare, two of my best friends from my club team play at [College X], and they have a male coach there. And they hate him. He buys plane tickets for them to go home because he tells them they suck every time. My friend was two minutes late and she got suspended. He tells them that they're the worst, and they hate going to practice and everything. But they had a great season last year. They beat [Team S]. I don't know, they said that they hate him, but they enjoy the sport and they enjoy winning.

Another D2 f/athlete said:

But Coach's expectations for us are sometimes masked by what she thinks we're able to do rather than just expectations of us as a team together. And she expects things individually to happen, whether you have to score goals, you personally, or you have to defend this girl one [on] one, like that's your mark. Whereas I feel like sometimes expectations as a soccer team should be just as a soccer team. Like expectations to win should just be a given. You should be expected to win every game because that's what you came out there to do in that 90 minutes.

Another D2 woman added:

About the expectation thing, every coach expects their team to win, except it's how you go about it, like we didn't win and then after every game it was just like, "It's a learning experience." Whereas some guys' coaches would have been, "This isn't okay. It's not okay that you lost." So everyone wants to win, everyone has that expectation, but it's what you do with it.

At the end of the focus group, however, one D2 teammate declared that what happened on the field really had more to do with the team than the coach: "And collectively, as a group, we kind of have to sometimes leave [our coach] out of it and just focus on ourselves, because we can do this together and we can win games together, we just have to remember that it's us, not Coach, on the field."

I wondered if many of these D2 players' frustrations were really not about their female coach at all, but more about their difficult prior season, lack of wins, and volatile team dynamics (talked about in depth later in this chapter). Such findings raise interesting questions about player and coach dynamics and influence.

Yet, it wasn't just with coaches that the f/athletes felt they had poor communication or a lack of respect. One D3 player noted that f/athletes didn't feel particularly important even in conversations with other male friends or students:

> If you're talking about women's sports, just in a conversation with a guy friend, I feel belittled almost, just because they think that they're better than us. Faster, stronger. And we work just as hard in the weight room.

Her teammates chimed in in agreement. One player said:

> It's kind of frustrating because our team, especially, works their asses off, and some people don't see that. There aren't guys that come to watch our conditioning or weight room sessions. So it's frustrating.

The D2 girls echoed very similar themes. One D2 athlete put it this way:

> By playing a sport, we've been labeled tomboys. So we've already taken on that persona. Look at us, we're boys, we're escaping this emotional thing. We're getting out there, we're grinding out for the team. We can push each other around and it's kind of going against what we're trapped in as females, la, la, la, la, la, let's be dancers. No, we're soccer players! Look at me! Hit me, throw me to the ground, rub some mud on me! Like come on! And now it's like, "Oh sweetie, let me fix your

ponytail! And I'm like, no. No, let me pull my hair back, let me go." And now it's back to the girliness of it.

Her teammate echoed the feelings of inequality, even noting that she—ironically—shared in the sexist attitudes:

I think that guys' sports in general are considered more dominant, just because they're guys. They're bigger, faster, stronger, more intense, and more fun to watch. Girls kind of get that we're not as important. But we're trying just as hard and at the end of the game, we're just as sweaty as they are. We put just as much effort into it. It's like, guys are faster but you're stronger so it's more intense and that's what everyone likes. Like I would rather go to a guys' basketball game than a girls' basketball game. I would rather watch a guys' anything, because it's more fun to watch, so I think everyone treats it that way too.

Another D2 player raised an important point beyond the physicality component to the intangible notion of expectations and reputation:

I guess just like, we're known to not be a good team, I guess. And the boys are. And they're a winning team and they made playoffs last year. I wish we could have a reputation similar to the boys at times, when it's on-the-field conduct. We deserve to be a winning team and we can be as good as the boys. We aren't pushed like [their coach] pushes them. I don't think we've been told we're really good, that we're good enough to beat this team. It's like, if we beat this team, that's huge for us. It's not

like, we're gonna beat this team, they should be scared
of us because we're better.

Such findings resonate very strongly with almost identical
comments from the middle and high school respondents. One D2
collegiate athlete said:

> The boys get more attention. Just look at the fans that
> go to girls' games and boys' games. So we could take
> yesterday, there was a boys' basketball game and a
> girls' basketball game. And there were definitely a
> lot more fans at the boys' game. And I wouldn't say
> the boys are better, because they're kind of not really
> good. I mean I could understand if they were better than
> the girls, maybe have more fans because it's a more
> competitive game, but they really aren't better than the
> girls, so... I guess there would be no reason why there
> should be more fans at one than the other. I just think
> there's a different intensity to it. Like even I was saying,
> I remember yesterday I was saying girls' basketball is
> so painful to watch, it's just so much slower.

A D3 athlete noted the differences in who shows up to games:
"Most of the male athletes here, not just on the soccer team or
whatever, they could not care less about coming to our games."
Her teammate added "True. I think the only ones that really do
are the soccer [players], and even then they only come for half
the time because they have practice or a game right after. That's
the other thing: I feel like we will always get the 4:30 game, but
the guys get the night game." A woman in the D3 focus group
added, "High school, college, we go first, we get the worst time."
It appeared to me that gender certainly played a significant role in

determining that girls' soccer is the warm-up act, while boys seem to be given the prime time.

One D3 woman recalled how powerful support of women's soccer can be:

> One of the games last year, or the year before, the football coach made the entire team go to our game, and that was one of our best things, it was awesome. We had such a big crowd, it was super exciting. And I remember some of the football guys saying that we played a great game. Like they were kind of surprised.

Her teammate added "And even though they were forced to go, they were having a great time," while another confirmed this saying, "They were into it and cheering."

One D2 player even felt the gender inequality extended beyond campus.

> There's no doubt they hype up a basketball game or a guys' hockey game more than a girls' soccer game. There's no doubt in my mind. Social media, posters.
>
> I'm from around here, but like the local papers, there's a little [college] blurb in there about women's soccer and then there's a huge blurb about men's soccer, even like men's hockey, men's basketball, and there's a little blurb about girl's hockey.

While the level of publicity illustrates the disparity between men's and women's soccer, ironically the women didn't always want to admit that gender was simply the critical factor here. One D2 teammate, when asked about why people seem to like men's games better replied, "I feel a part of it, though, is how the fans react. It's more intense because the fans make it more intense, if that makes any sense."

One D3 player though, put it most clearly when I asked why things were like this:

> Partially it's institutional sexism. Like kids grow up and are like, oh, let's watch the football game, let's watch the men's game! But never, oh let's go watch the women's games. Little kids grow up on that and it just becomes a habit.

One key event for the D3 players was when they went double overtime against the number one team in the conference. They were astounded at how well they had done. Unfortunately, they did not get the praise they hoped for. One woman said:

> I heard two people who were like, "Wow, you guys got lucky," and "You really had no business being on that field," and I was just like, "Okay, cool." Yeah, the team was awesome and it was a defensive game, but we still made them, for lack of a better word, shit their pants. Because they thought they were gonna stomp all over us and then when we came up and were 2-0; their coach was so scared. At halftime, we were winning 2-0.

One player interjected, "But to say that we were winning for 87 minutes, against the national champions—even though we didn't win, that's amazing."

One of the players added, "I heard maybe, I think it was in a class. This one teacher going 'Oh, and the girls' team, they did really good last night.' Blah, blah, blah, said all this stuff, and no one in the class said, 'Oh good job.'" Her teammate adds, "I feel like if it were the men's team, more students would have been talking about it."

Upon continuing our conversation, it became clear that most people on campus didn't even know about it, and, if they did, only wanted to know the result. One f/athlete responded, "But they didn't even recognize the fight that we had in the first half. Yeah, something happened and it got out of control and we didn't come up with the win, or the big W. But we were so close."

Clearly their season was outstanding, and yet they didn't feel applauded or validated in the ways they should have. As one woman said, "A lot of people disregard the fact that we were winning." Her teammate added the phrase used in this chapter title, "People are looking for the trophy, not the fight." Such a phrase is interesting in that it holds more than what it appears at face value. The women were arguing that the process mattered, not just the outcome. They believed that their training, teamwork, and perseverance were what marked them as f/athletes. Yet, what the majority of campus was saying was, "No, you don't matter as girls, and you didn't win." The almighty W seemingly overshadowed the process. One wonders if there is something here that speaks to the heart of gender in sport. Maybe, just maybe, the process matters as much as the W for women, which might not be true for men.

Such entrenched inequities about value and worth, in comparison to their male counterparts, are clear to these f/athletes, yet sadly they are not always sure how to make things better. What is interesting is that, compared to their younger female counterparts, I assumed that these collegiate athletes would have more rigid and well-formed ideas of how to solve such problems, yet they, too, seem to raise their open hands as if to say, "Why is this happening?" In both age categories, the young women easily pinpoint the disparities, but seem shocked that they are even there. Such findings relate to my earlier comments about girls being told they can be *anything* in a world that doesn't allow them *everything*. So I ask, are we raising a generation of girls that is going to hit lower glass ceilings than expected, encounter more closed doors, or be excluded from more hushed conversations? Will such toxic environments make them frustrated or determined? One can only hope the latter is true, yet I worry that might not be the case. I should be clear here that I am arguing that we tell girls that they can do great things and accomplish anything, but that we raise them with a clear sense of how structured inequities exist and have to be wrestled with[17]. Then, and only then, will girls arrive at adulthood not so flummoxed and dumbfounded by the entrenched sexism that exists there, but hopefully with battle armor on and strategies amassed for how to face such horrible, blatant gender inequities.

Beyond the sheer differential treatment of female athletes in comparison to their male counterparts, these collegiate f/athletes also face sexual discrimination.

---

17 Conversations about institutional discrimination—such as pay, hiring, and promotion inequities—coupled with discussions about unequal power and resources would be valuable information for girls to have. I am not arguing such discussions, however, take place on, or near, the soccer field, but, rather, beyond that space.

F/ATHLETES AS SEXUALIZED BODIES

The players noted that in some instances people watch women and sports, not because of how well they play, but because of how they look. One D3 f/athlete said:

> And when they talk about the team, they don't talk about how good they are, they talk about their looks and stuff. Like [professional player] Alex Morgan, they're always like, "She's beautiful." Why are they always talking about her looks, rather than how she can drive a goal? Why are you always talking about our looks? And it makes me think, why are people watching? Are they just watching because, "Oh, Alex Morgan's hot so I'm gonna watch it"? Watch it because we're good, and we play the game well.

What is interesting, though, is that when I pushed them about things such as why Ali Krieger, a USWNT player, had posed nude for the 2015 *ESPN* body issue, they respond not with criticism (which I expected), but praise for her athletic body. Comments included, "That's a personal choice. You are proud of your body," "Because she's worked hard to have the body that she has," "Her strong, muscular body makes her the great athlete that she is," and "Maybe it's more that she wants people to see that she is strong and muscular. It's not just like some model's body. She has curves, she has muscles, yet she's still beautiful." One D3 teammate noted, "I feel like if David Beckham posed nude, it wouldn't be as big of a deal," while another added "She could also have been even forced to do it. Like if you want to be in this cover shoot, you have to pose like this." Yet it was another f/athlete who summed up the complexities of bodies and identities by linking how the viewers' process of gazing actually shapes how both player and viewer conceptualize the athletes themselves. Each gender, she argued, watches for different reasons, with different experiential outcomes[18].

> It's definitely in how you look at it. I mean, she posed nude and someone looked at it like, "Oh wow, she's super hot, I should watch the games more often." Or you could look at it as, "Oh my God, she looks so strong, and I want to be just like her." It's more that people look up to her, like an I-want-to-be-just-like-her kind of thing. For other women—soccer players like us—when we watch the women's soccer team, we look up to them and want to be like them. But men who watch the team are, "Oh they're so hot," or talk about the little dramas, like Hope Solo and her husband and stuff like that.

Beyond talking about national players or celebrities, however, the f/athletes I met (particularly the D3 players) also faced blatant sexual discrimination themselves.

One f/athlete started the conversation:

> Okay. I don't know if everyone else has seen it, but when we were talking about the women's national team

---

18   Such findings remind me of a conversation I recently had with five female students in the few minutes prior to the start of my race and ethnicity class. I was asking about their prior evening, and they (all largely feminists) were recounting that they had watched the Victoria's Secret fashion show. I was shocked and surprised, noting to them that I assumed males would be the primary viewers, to which they replied, "Mostly women watch it, because they want to see how incredible the bodies are."

being oversexualized and stuff, all I could think about was how this team—I don't know if other people notice it—but on Yik Yak, people have called the women's soccer team, as a group, sluts, and been like, "Oh they're so hot."

I wasn't sure what she was talking about, and asked "This team? They called you sluts?" Her reply was clear, "Yeah. There was this specific Yak and they're like, 'Number seven is so sexy.'" Being completely out of touch with Yik Yak (thankfully), I asked, "What's that you're saying? What does it mean?" A player answered:

Yik Yak, it's like a random, anonymous, [now defunct] Twitter. You don't know who says it. Wherever you are, the location of it, so since we're on campus, everyone's Yik Yaks that they have out, everyone can see it.

Another teammate piped up, "It's like bullying online. Anonymous online bullying." Still another adds, "It could be as casual as, 'Great weather today.' Or it could be as bad as 'D3 slutty team, somebody getting arrested.'" A third teammate added, "It's been said multiple times, and I get heated about slut shaming. The second thing I get heated about is slut shaming." When I asked her "What's the first?" she replied:

Sexism. Sexism in general and then slut shaming. And it drives me insane that first of all, we're all grouped like that. We're individual people. Second of all, why are you calling us sluts for any reason? I don't care how many people you sleep with, it doesn't make you a slut. I hate that word. It's a shit word. But the fact is that we're not thought of as an athletic team—we're thought of how we are sexually, or how attractive we are.

For these f/athletes, showing one's body was a positive revelation of how hard they had worked to achieve such athletic definition. As one player put it, "Yeah, if we're packing, why not show it?"

It was clear that they associated a toned body with athleticism, and not just random good looks. One woman said, "Some people wear crop tops and show their stomach, and I think that's what they're basing it off of. They don't come to our games, so they don't refer to us as athletic or good at soccer. Like, look at her flat stomach, she's wearing a crop top, damn, I want to look like that."

One D3 woman summed up their frustration:

Yeah, I got a six-pack and I'm gonna show it. Oh my God, I'm pissed now. That's just ridiculous. That drives me insane... I don't understand why it's so goddamn important and we shouldn't have to conform so people don't think we're sluts. I shouldn't have to wear a turtleneck to a party so people don't call me a slut. That's ridiculous.

What is unique from these findings is that these collegiate f/athletes don't like their bodies being sexualized, but view commercialized images of women as different. On the one hand, this seemed like a paradox, yet I think it speaks to a more important facet of their gendered experience, which is that female athletes want the ability to define how their bodies are seen in different contexts.

MARKED IMAGE ON CAMPUS: POSITIVE AND NEGATIVE

All the f/athletes felt that being part of a team was critical to their identity. Several of them mentioned that it means you are part of something. One D3 player said, "I think it's a team legacy kind of thing too. We are confident and we take pride in being the hardest working girls' team on campus." A teammate added how it often ends up being a conversation starter. She noted, "When you meet someone new on campus and you're like, I'm on the women's soccer team." Sometimes the accolades from being a f/athlete are positive. One woman recounted:

> It's nice too, because we've had a couple of big games this past season. We went into double overtime with the national champions, and I had a teacher that stopped in front of the whole class and called us out and was like, "I just want to acknowledge this soccer team." And if we win, our faculty and staff are there, and you just feel like you're proud to be part of this great team and organization.

They also understood themselves beyond the classroom, and beyond how others saw them. One woman mentioned:

> I think it's also what we do off the field as well that makes us feel important, the difference that we make. This past year, we went to Ronald McDonald House in Mount Pleasant and were able to make a difference for the families there. That makes me feel important, that I can do that.

It is no surprise to me that, just like the collegiate coaches, these f/athletes want to make a difference in the lives of others.

Other players found that being an athlete certainly gave one an identity, but that it wasn't always what they wanted it to be:

> I feel like people respect us as athletes, but not for the game we play maybe. Maybe we're respected like, yeah, we work hard—on and off the field—but they don't come to our games, they don't want to acknowledge that maybe we actually are good athletes.

Others agreed, noting "I feel like we're important in that people are like, 'Oh yeah, they're college athletes, and only so few people make it that far,'" yet often the players clarified who was giving them the credit.

> It's people our age too, we're talking about those comments. I think it's like more our age group that will make those comments, rather than—obviously the administration has our back and are really supportive of us—and maybe it's non-athletes too that we get—I feel like the male athletes respect us more than just males around campus.

The f/athletes recognized that general sexism existed, but pointed out nuanced differences between their male soccer counterparts and male non-athletes. Such findings are critical in acknowledging variations amongst gender groups. Such details point to the intricacy of the world and our gender interactions:

I feel the boys have more respect for us than the non-athletes, because we do the same workouts that they do. They might not physically see it happening, but they know we do the same workouts they do. They know how much effort we put in to do what we do, and the regular students don't see it. They don't pass us in the hallway post-workout when we're disgusting human beings covered in sweat, and they don't see that, they don't see the amount of work and effort we put into being as good as we are... They don't think we work that hard.

For the f/athletes, their marked identity on campus not only targeted them with regard to being part of a team, but the f/athletes revealed that being on the team also meant being a second-class athlete as a woman.

There were two interesting ways that such inequality showed up on campuses, both relating to the use of physical spaces. The D3 team was very upset that they didn't have equality in terms of resources:

Okay, so basically, the men's teams have separate locker rooms. So the past two years, we've had one of the big locker rooms over in this hallway here. But every two years, we have to switch with the field hockey team into the smaller locker room, but the men's teams don't have to switch lockers ever. So this next coming year, we have to switch and go to the smaller locker room, and we have, how many people coming in?

Another teammate answered:

> At least 30. We have at least 30 girls on the team next
> year. At least 12 freshmen coming in and we have 20
> right now. But the locker rooms are so small, to the point
> where we can't do our normal rally, get ready, and pump
> up for game day. We have to go someplace else.

The players revealed that they end up having to share lockers,
and that there often isn't enough room for everyone to be in there
prepping before a game. The years they do have the big locker
room, the women note that the lockers were nice and actually so
large that you could fit your body in it. The smaller locker room
has lockers that are only 6 inches wide. They also complained that
the visiting locker room at their institution is nicer than the small
locker room they often are relegated to. When I told them that I
had seen a visiting men's lacrosse team coming out of the visitor
locker room, prior to our focus group, they said, "Yeah, that's a
big locker room. And it's only used by men."

In addition, they often felt (much like the young middle school
respondents) that they were given less desirable times for practice.
As one D3 f/athlete put it:

> Well, to bring it up again, the time slots that they get for
> games. They get the night games, we don't. They get
> the better times for practices. I can rarely think of a time
> when the men's team was practicing 9-11 at night, and
> we were.

Her teammates add, "They get the better workout times too," and
"We have workouts at six in the morning, and they have midday,

like 12:15 to 1:30." As our conversation evolved, it became evident that they were getting up early four times per week, and simultaneously having practices from 9:00 to 11:00 at night. What is interesting in this case is that this D3 institution has a female AD and yet women seemingly were not being treated equally to the men.

On a different subject, the D3 women also felt that there was no equality when it came to pre-game music on the field:

> It's a little bit smaller, but we talk about the music before games. For our team, it's really low and on the field, we can't hear it. For the men's team, especially football, it's super loud.

They recounted to me that on several occasions they had tried to get the problem remedied, but the excuse was always, "It's too loud." One f/athlete adds, "Actually one game I remember, it was loud and we were like, 'Oh this is a great volume.' And then it got turned down that same game." Sadly, one teammate remarked, "It's like someone called and they were like, 'Oh, the women's team is playing, make sure you turn that down.' "

Interestingly, they went on to tell me that they think it's because their games are during the school day. As one woman put it, "Well, maybe it's because we get such crappy times that people are still in school." Her teammates added, "Maybe if they heard loud music, they'd be like, 'Oh, there's a game going on, let's go watch it.' "

Despite being "just a girls' game," and the inequity in locker rooms, playing schedules and music, these f/athletes were shockingly resilient, strong, and bonded. The D3 team often spoke of themselves as family. Family is a pretty strong word for a bond within a team.

SENSE OF FAMILY

Both of the teams felt that they were family, more specifically as fictive kin—close friends that are thought of as family—yet there were nuanced differences between the teams as to how they construed such ties. For the D3 girls that I met, the kinship ties were a holistic part of their experience, which was fostered, in many ways, by the coach. The D2 girls, on the other hand, felt that they had to build those connections and links through struggle and perseverance. One fictive kinship model was not better than another; they were simply different based upon how they became constructed.

The D3 girls were really unique in terms of their bonds. I was struck by their dynamic energy, camaraderie, and relationships from the moment they entered the conference room where we held the focus group. Their comments exuded strong feelings about each other, no matter what age or position they played:

> I get to come in here and play with my ten best friends on the field and then have my other best friends off the field. Being there and knowing that they're cheering, it's just so amazing to have that bond that I've never had before. To play something that I love with the 20-something girls that I love is the best thing in the world.

Yet, beyond the love for teammates, the women knew that playing as a collegiate f/athlete gave them a unique opportunity shared by few women in college. One player added:

I think at least for me, I wouldn't be able to make friends like this, at all. These girls are my sisters and I'm gonna know these girls for the rest of my life, where like, I wouldn't know them. Me graduating next year, I'm gonna follow all of them and make sure they're doing awesome.

Her teammate added:

I transferred and the other team that I transferred from, we weren't close. Everyone hated each other—hated each other! And to come here was such a relief—to actually have people that played for the same thing and that loved each other, because it was awful [before].

What struck me most about these young millennials is that they understood that every person in this unique family had a role and that no one was more important than another, despite different positions on the team. One D3 player emphasized:

Every single person on this team has a role, and it doesn't matter if you're playing or not. I know sometimes if I'm down, I'll hear Vick and she picks me up. She has pushed me so much and it's just every single person has that role; it doesn't matter if you play 90 minutes or you play 2. You could be that spark to come in—and I think our team does a good job of recognizing that. It's not just the players on the field; it's every single person on our team that we play for.

Her teammate said:

We do outside stuff too. We do team dinners, we went apple picking. And yeah, we're college kids, we go out but we go out as a team. People refer to us as a pack, a herd, because whenever we come in or go to dinner, we all make sure we go together. We make sure no one feels left out.

The woman sitting near her added, "Or if one person shows up, you better be watching for the rest of the team!"

In some ways I was surprised by their strong positive, effervescent energy, and yet I also found myself questioning if this was just too perfect. Was I missing something? I prodded them with similar questions. Their responses seemed honest and in many ways parent-like. It appeared that they have problems, make mistakes, and apologize for them:

Yeah, we've definitely had some rough patches. We'll get frustrated during practices, but then after, you know, you see someone and be like, "I'm sorry I yelled at you during practice." Obviously we don't take it to heart or anything. We're like, "No, I understand, it was a rough day, you have so much to do." Or if you got upset, we'll text people and we're just there for each other. No matter what it's about, like boyfriends, families, or stressing out with school.

I soon came to figure out, though, that their male coach had built this program to have this specific family dynamic and he would not let it falter at any cost. One very interesting team-building project he had the f/athletes engage in was a wall project. One player explained it to me this way:

So, last preseason, this past one, he gave us a homework assignment. After practice, like three days later, we were gonna have a team meeting and we were gonna share our homework assignment. So we all went home and we had to make a personal brick. He gave us all a block, like a legit brick, and we had to decorate it however we wanted, and write a personal goal and a team goal on it. So then, when we came back, we were in this room to share our brick and each person took a turn saying their personal goal and their team goal. And the challenge was to try—we didn't really succeed at it. [Our coach] wanted us to lay the bricks in a way that couldn't be knocked over, no matter what.

Players began talking over each other in animated voices, "They all had to be touching or something," "We had to connect them and when we made it, it was not supposed to fall over, and if one brick is out of place, then the team—" She cut herself off mid-sentence as the players all noticed someone walking by the conference room. They began to yell and wave. I asked, "Is she on the team?" to which a player responded, "Yeah, it's always exciting to see our teammates around." A teammate interjected, "We're always like, 'oh my God'! Like we haven't seen them in forever." I realized from the conversation and this quick distraction that they clearly cared about each other, and acted toward one another in close, friendly ways. After their teammate was out of sight, they returned to discussing the wall project:

We could build the wall however we wanted, as long as you couldn't knock one part of it over, because if something happens on the team, if one person falls, the whole team falls down.

As one girl put it, he told them to create a foundation. Ironically, the girls tell me they had engaged in building the wall in the same room where we were holding our focus group:

We built it straight up, but he said, it can still tip over. If you were to pull it like this, some parts would come off. We had this great conversation. He initiated a conversation between us to recognize us, to remind us what each person is about and what we are about as a team.

Finally, one f/athlete added, "We kept it in our locker room for the whole year."

The symbolism of the wall project was not lost on the girls or myself. Yet, as our conversation ensued, it became obvious that their coach was critical in all of this culture creation. One girl put it this way:

Our assistant coach and our GA and our head coach are all on the same page. They call themselves the brain trust. I think they lay the groundwork and they ask us to hold each other to the standard that we're all in this together, basically. And then it's on us to focus, remember we want to win the [conference] and that's why we're all here.

They went on to share that he includes them in his private life, which the players recognize is crucial to feeling accepted and understood by him:

I think it also helps that he brings us into his own family. He invites us over to his house for team dinners. We spend time with his son. His son loves spending time with us, we love spending time with him. I think just the fact that he invites us into his home and treats us like his own kids almost. I think that helps us become a family even more.

A teammate added:

> I know when we lost this year, he texted the seniors and he was like, "I've never been so hurt because you guys are like my daughters, I treat you guys like my daughters." And it was something that was so touching—that he cares that much and was that upset. I know he feels that way for everything. He would do absolutely anything and he just does way more than a typical coach does. He gives his heart and soul for us because he believes in us, and that's the biggest thing. He believes in us when we don't believe in ourselves.

Yet more than just inviting them in to his personal space, he also had an honesty in his dealings with them. They shared that their male coach would tell them that they suck in games if, in fact, they aren't playing well. He also relies upon his female assistant coach; as the players put it, "They both play good cop, bad cop, depending on the game and how they're feeling about it." One player immediately added, "I'm kind of glad that we have kind of a softer coach now."

Not being certain what she was talking about, I asked, "Are you referring to the male coach or the female assistant coach?" She responded, "Just both of them, and in general, a softer coaching staff. Because we're trying to have fun and we play D3—it's not like it needs to be as cutthroat as a D1." Her teammate chimed in quite quickly, "But it still is for them. [They] take it very seriously." The first respondent acquiesced, "Oh yeah, they want us to be as serious as possible. I guess I don't know what I was trying to say." Such details about the characteristics they want in a coach—attitude, sensitivity, and compassion—reflect the same paradox echoed by middle school girls who want a coach to be tough, yet caring, what they called the "frotivator" (see chapter 5).

One key idea that arose during the D3 focus group was that their coach recruits people, not players. As one woman put it, "Yes, he wants the talent there, but he's also looking at each of our personalities and how we fit as a team. Like if he thinks someone is going to be a part of the team, but they're gonna just destroy us and take away that family and the care for each other, he's probably gonna just let them go." In fact, they recounted that in the previous year there had been a recruit who did not have a personality that fit the team. The coach asked them as a group what they thought, and they all said no to her, so she wasn't asked to join the team.

Before I left the campus they told me that they had been working on a team contract that outlined goals and how they want to treat each other. One woman shared:

> One of the things that we said is understanding constructive criticism and just being able to take—say I was telling Christina to step harder, to do something— it's not that I'm mad at her, it's not that I'm saying she's a bad player, I'm just trying to [help] - so I think that understanding constructive criticism—being able to take it and not feel like we're attacking you.

Her teammate added:

> I think that comes back to us being such a family again. We're not afraid to ask each other. If I start playing a new position this year and I don't know what to do—I was asking Judi, she's another senior on our team who

graduates this year what I should be doing. I wasn't intimidated or scared. I'm not scared of anyone on the team and the incoming freshmen shouldn't be either. We just want to help make each other better, we don't want to tear each other down or make each other feel horrible. We want to make each other feel good and great.

We've always emphasized how it's about the team—we not me—and I think it really helps that we've taken the time to get to know each other well enough that if I can tell Jo had a bad day, I'm not gonna annoy her on that day. I'll wait until another day to do it. We understand when each other is maybe not about really talking that day, or whatever.

Just as I was completing the focus group, they revealed that the male soccer players on their campus all get tattoos that say "family," but the girls aren't convinced of the value of the permanent markings. As one woman said, "They may get their silly family tattoo, but they're not a family like we are." In many ways, they are probably right.

In comparison, the D2 players also saw their teammates as family. They used similar phrases as their D3 counterparts:

We're literally like a family. We spend so much time together. Family dinners, family everything. My best friends are the freshmen on this team. [One teammate begins to cry.]

I asked them what else they do together that makes them a family, and they started to list things, talking over each other quickly and animatedly, as the comments flowed out:

War and Cleats

- *Homework.*

- *Everything.*

- *Life.*

- *Literally, I went to breakfast this morning with these guys. We'll hang out at night, do homework together. We'll goof around together, work out together.*

- *I found my roommate through soccer.*

- *We wear each other's clothes.*

- *I came back last night and I didn't even know some of them were wearing my clothes.*

- *Just sisters.*

- *We're probably as close as, if not closer than, the boys' team. Because we are way close, like almost weirdly close.*

- *Like, they call my mom, Mom.*

- *I talk to her sister on FaceTime sometimes.*

- *Yeah, I talk to her brother all the time.*

- *We have each other as family when we're here, but we have each other's families too. Like when their parents come up, we'll go out with them sometimes.*

- *Honestly, I think it would hate it here if it weren't for the friends.*

In some ways their comments sounded incredibly similar to those of the D3 players, but upon closer reflection it became obvious that their relationships and athletic journeys had been more strained and difficult. When I asked a graduating D2 senior if they were a family, she replied with a smile:

> Yeah, a family where you see your weird distant cousins every day. You put a bunch of people on a team that probably wouldn't have met if it wasn't for the sport. But you love each other and you're a family because you see each other too often to hold grudges.

It was clear that this group of fictive kin had a more complex set of relationships. Upon further discussion, it appears that their present coach had only recruited the freshmen and sophomores, and the upperclassmen had been recruited by, and played for, a previous coach. Such divisions, both in playing style and team camaraderie, were difficult for these women to navigate. One D2 player shared that after the older cohorts moved on, the team began to gain some positive chemistry:

> I think coming here and being on the soccer team, you have like a built-in family. So I think that's very refreshing, you have people you can go to and talk to. It's like a new start for everyone. I mean, it is college but it's a new experience. So I think it's refreshing to meet new people, to get to know your coaches, even though there are challenges. I think this year, we have a lot going for us. It's refreshing

especially with a lot of seniors leaving. It's a lot of weight off everyone's back, I think. It was a lot of pressure and I think now, everyone will be able to play their game.

Yet, prior to those older cohort groups leaving, the family felt fractured and full of dissonance. One D2 f/athlete commented that she was feeling anxious during our focus group as we were sitting in a conference room where some uncomfortable conversations had taken place:

I just think of the time we walked in [here] and everyone was crying and the seniors and [the coach] were in here and they got in this huge fight and it was right before a game, and they were like, "Okay you can come in" and everyone's in tears. All the seniors were crying and we didn't know what had happened. I think it's because [our coach] basically told them that they were the most disrespectful people she's ever met.

Such dynamics made for team instability and tentativeness on and off the field. Unfortunately, the drama with the seniors tainted their campus reputations. As one teammate put it, "Sometimes I go to boys that are on the men's team and say, 'Oh, this happened at practice.' And they're like, 'Oh, just the crazy girls, the women's soccer team.'" Sadly, the negative team dynamics spilled over into their lives off the pitch. A D2 teammate added:

If you watch the men's soccer team, you would never know who was in which class. If you watch the women's team you would be able to be like, upper classmen, underclassmen. You would be able to tell. It's like body language too. You'll see them, when they're out. Men will be all together, having fun. But if I see a senior at a party—yeah, you'll get the up-and-down look, with their drink in their hand. But I just don't care.

The players knew that the drama wasn't helping, but it wasn't until a core group of seniors left that social relationships and bonds improved. What was remarkable was that the then-sophomore class, who had been freshmen under that difficult senior group, stepped up to change the team dynamics. As one athlete put it, "They took every single one of us in and took care of us. And I think that goes off of how bad a freshman year they had. They made a huge point of making sure that we didn't have the same experience and I give them so much credit for that." Her D2 teammate added "The sophomore class brought the freshman class in. Under their wings." Their comments reflected the paradigm shift for these f/athletes.

A D2 teammate interjected:

> It's like actually super-bizarre that our chemistry is so good, as a collective group. I mean, we fight with each other and we say stuff that we regret—we all say stuff that we shouldn't—but at the end of the day, I'm gonna have your back against anybody else, and I think we are all so close because of how our seasons have gone. Because no one else understands what we've gone through as a group. If we didn't have each other, this team probably wouldn't exist, I don't think.

While another D2 f/athlete added:

> One of our seniors, it was the last game for them this season, and she's like, "I've been a part of a losing team

and it was this losing team before just the new group of girls, but this season didn't feel like a losing one." And she's an awesome player, she's one of my role models in life, she's just a great person. And for her to say that, I was like, "Wow, I can't wait to be a senior and have so much passion for the game."

At the end of the focus group, one teammate summed it up perfectly:

I just hope it's inspiring to the generation below us. That girls want to be like us. Because we were all the little girl in soccer once, with our cleats on. So I hope everybody else is looking at the same dream. Because there is a dream out there. We're kind of living it, I guess.

What is remarkable about these young f/athletes is that although they faced troubling gender microaggressions—particularly microinsults and microinvalidations—they rallied around each other to make bad situations more bearable. Returning to David Brooks' notions of what people need for a fulfilling life (see chapter 1), "doing gender" for these young athletes meant they faced their individual fears and stereotypes about themselves from others, and eventually crashed through such negativity. These young women were not going to go down without a fight, so to speak. They had grit, tenacity, and perseverance. In turn, they were not driven to give up or to succumb to people's stereotypes about f/athletes, but rather they found power and strength in numbers. Such findings point to the positive power of sports, and the efficacy it can have in young women's lives.

I now turn to the coaches I met who show similar levels of grit and tenacity in even more complex male-dominated environments. These women, too, show that females in sport not only face multi-layered battles about identity and capability, but rely on internal resources and in many cases, lean heavily on external resources (again relating to David Brooks' concepts in chapter 1) to cope with such cultural battles.

Chapter 5

Female Collegiate Coaches and Administrators: Coaching as Vocation in a Chilly Soccer Climate: Exploring the Behavioral, Relational, and Professional Influences on Female Soccer Players

Today, nearly half of the 3 million soccer players in America are girls, and in fact there are now nearly three times more female soccer players in the U.S. than there are Girl Scouts. (Haner, p.175)

The number of female soccer athletes in America is skyrocketing, yet the number of female soccer coaches is lower than it was before Title IX in 1972. In a recent article by Rachel Stark in *Champion Magazine,* she notes that "in 1972, women coached more than 90% of women's teams, and today they coach fewer than half" (p. 1). Stark rightly asks, "Where are the women?"

This chapter, an analysis of in-depth qualitative interviews with 16 head female coaches of D1, D2, and D3 female soccer teams, indirectly answers part of Stark's question. While my work on coaches is only one small segment of my larger study of 80 additional middle school, high school, and collegiate athletes and dozens of additional informal conversations with state administrators, soccer coaches, parents and players, I believe their rich and detailed narratives are pivotal components of a fuller understanding of how women fare in the often male-dominated soccer world. My work on coaches addresses and moves beyond Stark's question of investigating *where* the women are to showing *how* women are negotiating their respective situated locations.

My framework is constructed around four questions:

• Why are so few female soccer teams coached by women?

• What are their experiences as coaches?

• What happens within their structural work environments to encourage their careers and support the arc of those careers?

• What keeps women coaching at the collegiate level, despite having few fellow female colleagues?

Ultimately this work begins to explore the experiences of female soccer coaches and unearths the varied and multi-layered pedagogies and strategies that these coaches create to survive in an often male-dominated soccer world. The coaches I met constructed their coaching pedagogy around three main areas of social influence upon their players:

• behavioral/gender boundaries,

• relational/culture construction, and

• professionalism as relates to long-term personhood.

My findings resonate closely with the work of Guylaine Demers (2007) that attempts to answer how the role model (i.e., the coach) exerts influence over her or his players, but moves beyond it to expose the coaches' detailed stories, attitudes, and experiences, revealing that they see their jobs as more than drills and games, more than the proverbial Xs and Os, but rather as a vocation, as a calling. This calling is focused around a vision of clearing the path for young female athletes. What is interesting is that, while making a difference or changing the landscape was key for all of the coaches, *how* they did it was varied and complex. Some of the coaches saw their role as one of micro-level intervener—more of a mothering and mentoring task—whereby they wanted to change the girls' agency and actions[19]. Others spoke less of a personal transformation and more about structural changes. Yet in both cases they were engaging, dynamic, vocal, and extremely open about their views on the relationship between gender and sport. Their seasoned years, striking pedigrees, and vast experiences in the soccer world—from rec soccer all the way up to head coaching positions—gave them a unique and valuable insight into the messy world of youth and collegiate soccer.

In 1982 Roberta Hall and Bernice Sandler first spoke of the "chilly climate," a term referring to the unequal environment in America's classrooms whereby women found themselves treated differently than their male counterparts. Hall and Sandler noted that women were devalued, stereotyped, given lower expectations, and faced blatant harassment. Sadly, their research

---

19   Some coaches were such nurturers in their spare time, too, working as caretakers to make extra money. Hannah was taking care of a 90-year-old woman, helping her with her daily needs, when she wasn't at the university or on the field coaching 19-year-old women. I never met a male coach that was engaged in such daily, selfless, unconditional caretaking.

also showed that it was not just male teachers that created such disparate conditions, but that women were also complicit in the deplorable treatment of other women (1982, p.5). Sandler argued that, "individually, by themselves, the behaviors are generally small and seemingly not important. But when they happen again and again, they constitute a pattern of behavior that dampens women's ambitions, their classroom participation, and their self-confidence" (2005, p. 1). I argue that their work is just as valuable today as it was 36 years ago, and that unfortunately little has changed. I find in my research that athletic departments are not that different from secondary education classrooms and thus American female soccer environs are in fact a new chilly climate in the 21st century.

RESEARCH PROCESS

Between April 2015 and May 2017, I engaged in 16 in-depth semi-structured interviews with D1, D2, and D3 coaches and administrators from across the country. Fifty percent of the coach interviews were face-to-face interviews held either in my home or at their respective institutions, while the other 50% were done in recorded phone interviews due to the inability to travel long distances across the country. Such methodological practices are now becoming quite common given frenetic modern schedules and the easy access to technological connections (see work of Carr & Worth 2001).

The female coaches that I interviewed have come up through the ranks, playing rec, club, high school, and collegiate soccer, eventually becoming full-time head coaches at well-known D1, D2, and D3 colleges and universities in every region of the country. Their untold stories are unique, engaging, and, in many ways, hopeful. When today's media outlets focus on successful female players, they turn to USWNT players, but little is ever discussed about other accomplished females in soccer—the collegiate coaches across the country—and how they see and experience the wonderful sport of soccer. NCAA data shows that women coach 40.1% of female NCAA teams across all sports. In contrast, my extensive national data collection shows that numbers of female soccer coaches for D1, D2, and D3 female soccer teams combined are sadly much, much lower, averaging only 28.4%[20].

My work shows that coaching is a fine, delicate balance of yearning for intrinsic transformation of self and player, nestled within the broader, intricate gender dance of sport in higher education[21]. Such a gender dance is found within the structural confines of athletic departments, higher educational battles over resources, and the contemporary broader discourse of gender and sport in the United States.

Women *want* to coach because as Barbara, one of the D2 coaches in the study, put it, "I want to make it right." Ella, a D3 coach kept coming back to the phrase, "I want them to be good humans." She told me that meant "to be good—to yourself and to other people— and learn how can we do that and be competitive and learn our sport, and do other things we love to do." These coaches want to make a difference, to be a role model (similar to findings by

---

20   See unpublished quantitative work of Maya E. Bhave and Jacquelyn Duffy "National Coaching Analysis: Female head coaches of Division I, II and III female soccer teams" May 2017, http://mmurl.de/nationalcoachinganalysis.

21   As such, my findings on the fluidity of gender resonate with Barrie Thorne's work on gender play in 1993.

Donna Pastore in 1991), and, at least in terms of my respondents, not because that seems right or trendy, proper or admirable. They want to coach because they see it as a calling to change the chilly climate they endured over the years within the male-dominated soccer world and to make it better for younger women below them in the hierarchy.

FINDINGS

COACHING AS A CALLING

All of the coaches I interviewed spoke passionately about how unique and important it was to be a collegiate female coach. Their stories were not negative diatribes, despite recounting a variety of difficulties of being female in male-dominated environments. Rather, the stories were often passionate statements about how much they loved the sport and engaging young women on and off the field. In this chapter, I outline how female coaches developed varied coaching pedagogies with a desire to decrease inequities for future generations by teaching them how best to survive as women in a male-dominated sport.

This calling moves beyond teaching young women the game of soccer; it is about building character. These coaches envision their work as fighting a battle they've already been a part of (one they didn't always win), and they want to make sure the next generation gets it done properly. Barbara explained, "It's not just telling someone to do something, it's actually living that life and being what you want, or what you deem important traits for other people to become." Coaching involves shaping girls' behavior and sense of self at three levels: behavioral, relational, and professional. Some women navigated their vocational terrain by using a symbolic interactionist vision connected to personhood, micro-level interactions, and symbolic events and conversations. Others tended to focus more on structural and formal changes in departments and institutions, battling with A.D.'s and fellow coaches for a shift for women. I should note that the separate approaches were actually not always clear cut and dichotomous. Women actually navigated the terrain much like Barrie Thorne's (1993) notion of gender play, in ways that were "fluid and contextual," (p. 159) as they found themselves weaving in and out of both sides—the personal and the political—while trying to impact these young women in powerful micro and macro approaches.

For these women, coaching reveals unique ways to "do gender."[22] Primarily, coaching is about their intrinsic desire to be seen, heard, and valued, and ultimately to create and encourage those same ideals in their players. Coaching consequently becomes a value-driven calling that moves beyond what some might call the traditional male-driven notion of Xs and Os. That is not to say these women aren't results driven—because they are—but they add another component to their job focus.

One typically doesn't think of sociology, Max Weber, and soccer in one sentence, yet his work on living for and off our vocation

---

22 It is extremely important to note that there are certainly male coaches who also see their role as one of being a mentor. When I informally asked a dozen male soccer coaches what their goals were in coaching, they used similar language: "growing people" and "making a difference." One might think that coaching is just coaching, but my work shows that women and girls don't perceive or experience their environments in the same ways as their male counterparts. Thus, how women make a difference in these climates is critical to understanding the broader boundaries of this ever-growing sport.

ends up being critical to my work (Gerth & Mills, p. 84). What is remarkable to me today is that deep within the distant, and complex, environs of the American soccer world, Max Weber's ideas and concepts of vocation and work still elicit valuable insight. Google the word *work* and you will get over 7 billion results, yet unearthing exactly what our work means to us is the tough job[23].

Listening and attuning themselves to the message of their calling was critical for all the coaches I met. No matter what division they coached in, whether they lived on the West Coast or the East, or were from the Northern plains, bayous, or swamp areas of the Southeast, they all had one focus: soccer was something they felt suited for and completely dedicated to. In fact, the first question in our interviews was always to fill in the blank in the sentence "Being a coach makes me feel _____."
The women responded quickly with words such as *empowered, fantastic, helpful, relatable, satisfied, impactful, unique,* and *proud.* Most often they used the word *empowered* and when I asked them to elaborate, they spoke eloquently and at length about what coaching gave to them.

The coaches felt that having a life that revolved around soccer meant one thing: impacting women far beyond the field. Emma, a D1 coach, called herself a "whole person educator doing work that matters," while her D1 counterpart, Mia, called coaching

---

23   In a 1998 Fast Company article entitled "Is Your Job Your Calling?" author Alan Webber documents Harvard Business School psychologist Timothy Butler's take on vocation. Butler states that "vocation is the most profound of the three, and it has to do with your calling. It's what you're doing in life that makes a difference for you, that builds meaning for you, that you can look back on in your later years to see the impact you've made on the world. A calling is something you have to listen for. You don't hear it once and then immediately recognize it. You've got to attune yourself to the message" (Webber, 2).

women "laying a foundation." Emma noted that she felt she was having an impact on girls' and women's lives, and that it was empowering for girls and women to realize their full potential and learn that they could do and achieve more than they ever thought they could. Kathy, a D3 coach, describes her calling this way:

> One thing that typically frustrates me is that people think that my job is just fun. You get to go out and kick a ball all day long and that's what I do. And I'm like, if my job was just coaching soccer, it would be so, so easy. Now, is it fun and rewarding in different ways? Absolutely. But those ways are much less about soccer and much more about people. For me, as much as I love soccer—and I really do love soccer—I see my job as more of a calling. If you imagine my job as a cake, soccer is the frosting on the cake, but the real meat and potatoes of it all is actually the cake. And I really believe that my calling is to be involved in the lives of 18- to 21-year-olds who are really beginning to make decisions about what their lives will look like, what their stances are on things (no longer just their parents' stance), and the choices they're making that will develop who they are. And being a part of that is probably the hardest and most rewarding part of my job.

What is critical to notice here is that they did not develop such attitudes in a vacuum, but rather from an implicit Weberian stance; they were shaped by their own personal, historical contexts and interpretations. It was clear that the female coaches I met often looked backward to look forward, meaning they were always responding very intimately to their own personal backgrounds. These women learned what was good or bad coaching by sifting through the traits of former coaches or athletic colleagues. Such people made strong impressions on them—in some cases, positively but, unfortunately, often negatively.

Barbara, for example, recounted the coach she played for when she first went to college and how that coach helped her respond to personal trials including a rape:

> So I think [Coach] did amazing by me. And what I would see from her is how much she had extended herself for me, and it wasn't even just me, I feel like she did it for the whole team, with the things that she did. Like I got in trouble in the dorm, and then I went to the hospital during preseason initiation for drinking too much. Then I got mad one day and put my fist through a window. Do you know what I mean? It was like "Oh my gosh, get out of your own way!" She had a vein pop out when she'd get mad, but she was awesome. Holy crap, was she intense. But she was awesome; it was good. Honestly, she was amazing. She really went out of her way and was really concerned for me. Even reached out to my parents at one point because of how down I was. Because you're faking it, being happy, and of course, I didn't tell my parents, but I told my coach. *That* I wasn't going to tell them.

That was a reference to being raped on one of her college scouting college visits at a different college. The one place (soccer) that Barbara thought she was safe, she found to be devastating. She went on to talk about the role of her coach in her life:

> And she was like in a balance of how to tell my parents she was worried about me and not tell them—but she did the best she could, I think, to help me. And I think—looking

back at it now—I think when you go through a traumatic experience, I think you have to figure out that time in your life when you can deal with it, and it wasn't then.

I must note here tangentially that within 16 qualitative coach interviews, I heard about three rapes of their female players. In one instance, there were two rapes of players on one team. Kathy, a D3 coach, recounted the difficulty of trying to help her grieving player:

> She texted me and all her text said was, "I don't necessarily want to talk about it, but something really bad has happened, I'm back home to get help." So I kind of left that alone, and then—this was the same spring break with the drinking, so someone else got arrested for underage possession of alcohol—I got stressed... so I just texted her back and said, "I know you don't want to talk about it and I'm good with that; I just need to know that everyone else is safe." And she said, "Yeah, everyone's safe," and that's when she started telling me the story. And since then, we've walked through it together for the remainder of the semester. She told her parents, obviously, and I've been in some communication with her parents, but that's it. It's a difficult line to tread, in that you know they can't tell their parents everything, that's just the way the world works sometimes. So I want her to be comfortable with the fact that the stuff she tells me, that I absolutely would not tell her parents.[24]

---

24 Mandatory reporters are individuals (ranging from teachers, clergy, child care workers, health care providers to social workers) who are mandated to report physical harm and sexual abuse (which includes rape) of any child under the age of 18 to the local department of child/family social services within 24-48 hours (in most states)

No matter whether it was Barbara talking about her rape years prior while being a high school student who was looking to play college soccer or listening to Kathy recount her perspective as a coach, I was deeply troubled by the narratives. Much more research needs to be focused on the percentages and experiences of f/athletes (and non-athletes) experiencing sexual violence on our college campuses.

Other coaches—like Mia, a D1 coach—also spoke passionately about the influence of their former female collegiate head coaches. Ironically, I had interviewed Mia's former coach, Emma, for this project, and Mia did not know that. Mia recounted that significant mentoring relationship:

> And honestly, so of much that goes to Emma and the experience I had, because she made me be the absolute best player I could ever become, and the absolute best leader, individual, just prepared for life, and honestly, she is ultimately what triggered me and allowed me to see the profession of coaching as a reality, particularly collegiate coaching. So I owe so much to her in why I am even standing here as a head coach now, so it was amazing.

It was interesting how many times women spoke about fellow players, coaches, or mentors who were already, unbeknownst

---

of suspecting or learning of the abuse or neglect. For college students over the age of 18, they can report such harm or abuse to their campus Title IX coordinator, who is not obligated to report it to parents, but will take action regarding the allegations. In addition, "responsible employees" are designated on campuses that must report allegations of sexual harassment/violence to the Title IX coordinator. As of Sept. 2017, this was the legal framework; however, as this manuscript was going in to the publication stage, Education Secretary Betsy DeVos noted that she would shortly release new information on who constitutes a "responsible employee" on campuses across the country. I was not able to include that new information here.

to them, involved in this project. I quickly recognized that such revelations were evidence that there are relatively few women within the American collegiate soccer domain. Such female social role clusters, therefore, end up being quite tight and small.

It is clear that, despite their small numbers, these female coaches play a significant role within collegiate athletics. These coaches do so much more than run drills and organize tournaments and matches. The coaches I met were so strongly impacted by their previous coaches who cared about them—not only as athletes, but also as young women. Katelyn, a D3 coach, told of a traffic accident she had years ago while driving her college coach to an adult league soccer game:

> We got hit by a drunk driver. We were going to a soccer game at 6 o'clock in the evening. She was the passenger, I was driving. The car stopped at a stop sign and I was going. Then he pulled out in front of me, and I tried to take the impact on myself and not her, but she ended up breaking her sternum and her foot, and having to get 10 stitches in her head. I just had a scar on my knee where the key went in. And I felt so bad. This was the year before my senior year. My fourth year of playing soccer. She said she was happy that I didn't get hurt, because then I didn't have to miss out on my senior year of soccer. She was okay with it. She wanted to see me play my senior year and not miss out.

I asked Katelyn why this felt so deeply important to her. She replied, "That was like, I give you my respect and I'm gonna give you everything that I got to give you, because of that." At this point in our interview, she began to tear up, overcome with emotion.

Katelyn also later mentioned that, when she began to work as a head coach, she used both the positive and negative coaching styles she had witnessed as fodder for best practice: "I've taken the experiences of me getting yelled at, the experiences of being on a program that wasn't so good, [and] the experiences of being in a program that was good."

In contrast, other women spoke passionately about how certain coaches had taught them exactly what they didn't want to emulate in their future careers. Sydney talked about her first undergraduate head coach who appeared callous, indifferent, and insensitive:

> I remember during preseason, all of us completely joking about how he would be, "Oh, how're you doing?" And you'd be like, "I don't know coach, I think I'm gonna die." And he'd be, "Oh great, see you later. "And I remember we were laughing so hard coming up with things we could tell him, but because he's never talking to you directly. You could say, "I think I'm dying." And he'd be, "Okay, great, great, great." I remember that one specifically because he was pretty atrocious.

She also talked about athletes having eating disorders:

> And they usually were built from him. He did this to one of my very good friends our freshman year. We went to him because we noticed she wasn't eating, and she was working out 2-3 times a day. And he told us, "Well maybe you should do that, too." So we say, "Something's not right, Coach." He was the

portal, as the coach, and he brushes us off. He said, "She's just working out hard, maybe you should do that, too."

Sydney realized immediately that this is not what a good coach should be like. Later, he saw the aforementioned friend's tiny, weakened frame—often hidden under big sweatshirts—and his response was, "You need to get control over your strength." Sydney found him abhorrent and later concluded that some men just don't value women in sports:

> I honestly feel like some men feel they can't coach other men, but [will] coach women because they're already second class. And I've heard—absolutely from the mouths of these people, so this isn't just conjecture— that they say, "Oh it's just girls." And they're coaching women's collegiate teams, for good pay!

For the coaches I interviewed, it was critical that they pave a path for younger women to experience the best that a soccer environment could be. Yet these coaches see their vocation as a calling, far beyond the Xs and Os of soccer. These female coaches, I believe, are trying to shape their athletes so they face fewer problems and gendered judgments later in life, given their own personal past experiences in chilly soccer environments. They want these young women to be more than sexualized bodies, second-class citizens, and voiceless females who cannot advocate for themselves. The coaches I met tended to focus on three main areas of social influence: behavioral and gender boundaries, relational and cultural construction, and professionalism and long-term personhood.

BEHAVIORAL AND GENDER BOUNDARIES

First and foremost, these coaches wanted to make sure that girls were respectful *to* others and respected *by* others. In many ways, they took on the role of life coaches to their players, as much of this teaching had little to do with soccer and more to do with surviving life as a woman[25].

Mia, a D1 coach, explained how her actions and attitudes impact her players:

> I take it really seriously and I think I show my passion. I think they're like, "Oh, this isn't just something she does, she's into it. She's all in." And again, I think when you embody those things and walk that walk, they can more easily follow suit. I think it's a 360-degree level of investment and it probably seems like just something you say—" Yeah, I'm all in"—but to me it's a lot deeper and to me it's a level of consistency when you're away from the field, away from the pitch, when you're in the classroom, when you're having to make hard social decisions, when it's just doing it, or really compelling yourself to do something. I think it's all those things and it's bigger than yourself—that's why it's 360 degrees and it's constant—you can't turn it on and turn it off.

---

25 The soccer world is a complicated gender terrain, as I pointed out earlier, in that the D2 college players in the previous chapter didn't always want a life coach, but rather just a coach that focused on athletics. The athletes' responses point to the varied and dynamic ways that gender impacts our lives and our broader views of being female. Similarly, coaches make sense of their own gender and identity in multilayered and varied ways.

I asked her if this happens organically and she said, "I think we can't just take it for granted that it would happen naturally." Thus, Mia purposefully plans how to impact her players. She divides them into groups that end up doing activities together both on and off the field, during preseason and beyond. Other coaches also focused on intently impacting the social and emotional behavior of their players.

Barbara, a D2 coach, remembered a player on her team who needed guidance about maturity, behavior, and words:

> It's funny, I have a captain who is probably one of the most mature players, but at the same time, she doesn't have the ability to advocate for herself. There was one point this year that she came to my office and very inappropriately spoke with me and didn't apologize for a situation that had happened, which was me pulling her off the field because she was playing horribly, and kind of how she spoke to me on the side of things. We addressed it and she didn't apologize and by the end of the conversation, she was basically saying, "I never speak up for myself and bah, bah, bah." And I was like, "Listen. There are ways to speak up for yourself and I appreciate what you're trying to do, but you need to find when and how to do it a lot better. And these are the ways you can do it." Because she had never done it before so it was coming across completely horrible and inappropriate and offensive and attacking, and so we just talked about that. And when I met with her again at the end of the season, we addressed it again, to just say, "Listen, your voice is important, but *how* you use your voice is even more important." And when can you

say this, when can you do that type of thing, and what's important and what's not.

Later Barbara added, "And I would say confidence is a huge thing that I'm trying to get for a lot of these young women as well, just being confident in [who] they are and the decisions they make, and that they should be proud of what they do." These coaches want their players to first and foremost learn about respect, advocacy, and professional boundaries. They believe that such traits will hold them in good stead on and off the field.

I should note that the administrators I met through the larger project also spoke passionately about conveying proper behavior and self-regulation. Sue, a former high school coach and soccer administrator, vividly recounted a conversation she had once on the way to a game:

> The teenage girls were in the back seat of the van, talking about a story that had come on the radio. We were hockey fans. I'm a [professional hockey team] fan. There was a [team] issue, some of the players had [been] accused of rape. They had met some girls in a bar, they went back to their hotel room, and the next day, the girls are crying rape. And so I said to my girls that were in the car, "This is something for you guys to think about. I'm not saying that those guys are innocent, but what I'm saying is, there's a level of personal responsibility here. And I'm gonna tell you right now, when a guy invites you to his hotel room, he's not looking to play checkers."

She wanted them to be mature, responsible, and respectable, and felt that she played a pivotal role in teaching them such valuable life lessons. She bristled at male coaches that she had met over the years who she felt had done little to help these girls' senses of self-confidence and autonomy:

> They were arrogant and I hated that [guy]. He just was so arrogant, and I can't tell you how many girls I've met since then that have said how awful it was playing for him. He just belittled them. I have a physician who I've gone to who said that she played for him, and she goes, "That man did his very best to destroy my self-esteem."

Sue wanted the world to be different for these girls, and was not going to take her job lightly. She worked tirelessly to make sure they understood how to better themselves beyond the athletic field:

> We had three rules: no talking when I'm talking, respect each other, and no whining. I had a T-shirt that I wore to practice that had *No Whining* crossed out in a circle. One of my players gave it to me. I wore it to practice all the time, I probably still have it.

Another woman I met, Annie, a D2 coach, recounted how she, too, taught her players about manners, appearance, social behavior, and community:

> Every year in preseason they have the welcome mass for all new students and whoever to kind of kick off the year. And when we went to that, we were actually pretty gross—we went straight from training so we were a little bit sweaty—and so we sat in the back and the whole team was there. The next day I got an email from a professor who said, "Oh my gosh, it was so great to

see your team at that mass, in your uniforms." I don't know if she thought we were in our game uniforms, but either way, she was like, "You guys looked great, it was great to see you there. Thanks for supporting." I'm a big believer that, yes, we are our own little entity, but we're part of a larger community and if we want people to come support us, we're gonna support them. It doesn't mean we're gonna go to every mass as a team—we don't—but we do go to at least the welcome mass as a team every year. So little things like that. I want us to be seen and I want people to say, "Oh, that's the women's soccer team" and obviously have it be positive in what their next thoughts are. But that means getting out there, being involved. Not just September to November—come to a game, but then the rest of the year we disappear. We love to volunteer, we love to get involved, we love to support other causes and athletic teams on campus. And that obviously was part of the culture as well. And I think the only difficulty I faced was just realizing how few resources I had, whether that was monetarily or facility-wise.

Sometimes the lessons that the coaches taught were more serious than just saying the right thing or being seen appropriately in the campus environment. Coach Katelyn recalled when a player came to her, terrified that she was pregnant:

You're in panic mode as a coach. And you're just like, "Oh God, oh God, oh God." So it ended up being okay and I had a long conversation with her afterwards, saying, "Look. You have to take control of yourself. You have to pay attention to what you're doing and if you're getting so far intoxicated that you don't know what you're doing, you gotta take yourself out of that situation." So she did, and she's moved on. She has a kid now, but she didn't during college, thank God. That's all I care about—under my care, you're good.

She recognized that although she wasn't really prepared to help a young woman in this predicament, Katelyn thought back on something a former coach had said to her:

And you're thinking, what am I gonna tell her? I have never been in that situation myself. And I'm just kind of going, "Oh my God, please say the right thing, please say the right thing." And I said to her "Okay, what do you want to do? What can I do to help you with this situation?" And she's like, "Well I don't need any help, I just need to figure this out." And I said, "Okay." I said, "How do you want to figure this out." I said, "You gotta let me know what's up, you know." And she said, "I think I just want to go to the doctor." And I said, "Do you want to do that now? Or do you want to do it later?" And she's like, "I don't know."

So thinking back to what [a former coach] had said to me when I was sick, I said to her, "I'm gonna leave the decision up to you." I said, "If you're gonna be here for practice, you gotta be here for practice. Or you can leave and do your thing." And she ended up leaving and doing her thing, which was totally fine with me. Because it was one of those things where it was like, "I can't judge you. I don't know how to deal with this situation, so I'm just going to go with the flow in this situation."

Clearly coaching is about helping young women make decisions, often to keep themselves safe. In other situations, though, coaches felt they needed to teach their athletes broader notions about team relationships and dynamics within the campus environment.

RELATIONAL AND CULTURAL FACTORS

Many coaches spoke about how their primary goal beyond player development was to create a team culture that helped young athletes relate better to teammates, staff, and the broader world around them. Some coaches, such as Ella, spoke passionately about trying to help women to become better socially, emotionally, and physically:

> This past year, we took a pretty big step in terms of having some really great leadership on the team, and really pushing being a part of something other than ourselves, and being a big family and having each other's backs, and taking that step to push ourselves as a team to be competitive and be better and expect more out of ourselves, and being okay with pushing ourselves to a certain extent and realizing that we can do more than what we thought we could do.

Ella elaborated that this culture was set by her and not by the team. She was the leader and thus her tone mattered:

> I'm not a yeller, I'm not gonna scream at you for making a mistake or two. We're gonna learn from it and we're gonna figure out, "Okay, what else can we do instead of that?" So I started being intentional in terms of how

I say things, in terms of my personal interactions with them and then with myself as well, setting my own intentions for the day as a coach: I get to be here and coach soccer and work with some amazing women, who get 4.0s in school that I'm proud of. So to remember that before I go and work with them, I think, helps a lot.

What is interesting about Ella is that she didn't always have this interactionist cultural framework (defined as one connected to personhood, micro-level interactions, and symbolic events and conversations) at her fingertips; rather she developed it after her own soul-searching adventure. Six months prior to speaking with me, Ella had hiked in a rural mountain range for sixteen and a half days by herself. Her experience had taught her a new outlook on her own life and, subsequently, on coaching. For Ella, coaching goes beyond the Xs and Os, and as such her life experiences as a woman directly shape that of her players:[26]

I've had a lot of time to think about it, but to be able to be sort of on your own in the middle of the woods— maybe specifically as a woman—and to just know, "Hey I'm gonna be able to do everything I need to do to get to the end of the trail." At the same time, there were stops where I had food drops and friends, and being able to spend a few hours restocking my bag

---

26 I should note that having a micro-level impact also is implemented by many male coaches, but the difference is the power environment that women find themselves in. Female coaches try to change lives in the midst of their own private or public battles for power. Men have fewer uphill battles to fight within this male-dominated sport. A future comparative study of male coaches does seem important, however, particularly as so many men have shaped these women's lives in positive and negative ways.

and talking to some really good friends, makes you realize that connection with other people is also pretty huge, in terms of giving you those mental boosts that you need. And I think that's something I didn't know. I've always been slightly more introverted and sort of independent, and like, I can do things on my own. But I think to be able to feel how important that connection with other people was made me much more—I'll go talk to anybody, anywhere, anytime now, more so than before I did the [hike]. My friends joke all the time that this is post-[hike] Ella. And I'm okay with it, it's great. So it was a pretty cool experience for me.

Ella had thought about doing the nearly 300-mile solo hike for about five years prior to taking on the challenge. One of the most interesting findings for her personally on the trek was what it meant she had to rely upon friends for food drop-offs:

It finally clicked that those connections are really important. Not that you didn't think they were important before, but to know that I actually could feel an energy boost from it, I felt better from it, and I could see how much it helped pretty immediately. It was pretty eye opening for me and something I could think about and now those are relationships that I want to fortify, as well as others. I want to go meet new people and I want to engage in conversations with others that I would just maybe not try before.

For other coaches developing this interactionist, micro-level culture, it was less about relationships and more about advocacy.

Coaches like Melanie agreed that their role as coaches is to empower, a term that many women said was what coaching really gives to them. Melanie, a vivacious D3 coach, talked about what being empowered meant to her:

> I think more so that I own my voice. I own my voice and I feel like I can use it, and I have a lot of power to influence others... We do a lot of Xs and Os and obviously that develops discipline and all those things on the field. We have so many sidebar conversations. We even have a joke that, "Well, that's a conversation you couldn't have if your head coach was a man."

When I pushed her to explain what these conversations are about and what she is trying to teach, she replied:

> I went to this women's conference once, and they were talking about how women have far more control globally than we realize, and that we control 80% of spending globally, because we control our household incomes for the most part. You're spending at Target, all that stuff. So your dollar is your vote. So you might feel powerless. We talk a lot about this, especially with the election, because I had a lot of kids that were—they weren't like, troubled by it, but they were like, "Oh my God, I have to become invested politically now." And so we talk about things like maybe we don't want to go march, maybe you don't want to call your senator, but you can be more conscious of where your dollar's going and send your message that way.

Later she adds:

We talk about just the little stuff like that all the time—
we do the spending one a lot, because they joke about
the fact that there is a Lululemon store that I will
not go to, because I didn't like the vibe when I went
there, and so it becomes our joke because I still shop
at Lululemon, but I will not give my money to that
particular store. And then that usually leads into my
older players being like, "Oh, that's right, cause we
control the money!"

Melanie finds that it is these off-the-field—often non-soccer—
moments that she calls sidebar conversations that shape her
athletes as much as any drill, set play, or penalty kick practice. She
recently took a team on a service-learning trip abroad, stating, "It
was incredible. My relationship with the team is far better now,
because they spent ten days with me, so you can't help but know
each other a little better." She argues that coaching allows her to
share her values and is about "redefining leadership," which for
her means teaching her players how to communicate with others
and to push their thinking beyond what they know. Such teaching
often conflates with doting roles that seem akin to mothering.
The women even say so. Melanie does, however, recognize that
students need different things at different times in their careers:

Some are gonna be vocal leaders, some that's never gonna
be their style. And I think redefining that has been helpful
for a lot of them. And the natural evolution in our program
has been, freshmen get—they still need me as a mother,
that's just part of what the role is to help them through this.
Sophomores, I tend to butt heads with the most, because
sophomores think they've got it figured out, but they
don't. So they're still not in charge, but they want a larger

say. For juniors, things start to go really well, and then when they're seniors, they basically run the team. I take so much input from my seniors. I see them as an extension of me as coach. I don't have a full-time assistant, so I feel that I have to rely on my players a lot to get things done.

Later Melanie tells me that she too has gone through an evolution of sorts, what she calls a "a spiritual evolution," in which she herself has become more approachable to her players and even more vulnerable. "Not to the point where we're friends, but letting them know that I've had failures in my life, or I've got dreams, stuff like that."

One D2 coach, Sydney, elaborates further, describing how coaching relates to creating unique bonds, much like a family. She noted:

Nothing compares to the sort of familial setting of being a woman coaching women. When I really think about that piece, I can't imagine getting that connection any other way, at least in my experience of the things I've done. I never felt that kind of connection, protection of the family, of the young ladies I work with, and being able to inspire and motivate, but you also want them to learn how to do it themselves. To believe in themselves and have that kind of deep connection. I never had [that] in any other capacity, ever.

Annie's comments resonated with those of Sydney, in terms of the notion of respect and identity:

Because I always go with the type of mentality that there's two types of people in this world—good people and not-so-good people—and I want these women to be good people. And that starts with accountability, it starts with being 15 minutes early to everything we do and dressing all the same. Everybody has the same practice gear, the same socks. Maybe that's a little bit of my OCD again, but you want to be proud to represent women's soccer and one of the things we say here is that you wear your jersey 24/7, even if you're out in jeans and a sweater; it's your identity, you're a women's soccer player, people know that about you, and you want to be proud of that. So I think that that was a lot of the underlying things, that pride, that integrity, that passion for what you do. We've always preached that you have four years to do this, so you're gonna do it right.

Clara, a D2 coach, spoke of the same kind of value in the idea of accountability. She shows up for the students' senior class presentations—such as a recent presentation on marine biology—that have no connection to soccer or sports. Yet Clara impacts girls far beyond the field and even beyond graduation:

I feel with the girls that it's a 24/7 job. I'm their coach, I'm their mother, I'm their big sister, I'm their counselor, I'm their friend. Sometimes I'm their disciplinarian.

Later she revealed an incredible story of one of her players whose sibling was killed in a U.S. military intervention abroad:

And I'm the one who gets the phone call. The mum called her, and they couldn't get through to her, so the parents called me, and now I've gotta go to the dorm, find the kid, sit with the kid while I tell the kid, "You need to answer your phone, your mum's about to call." We continued to help the kid through the grieving process, and a couple of weeks later when his body was flown back, we took two vans, we went to the funeral, we actually were sitting in the first three rows for the funeral. There [were] over a thousand people at this funeral because it was a military funeral. We were even addressed at the funeral. This is how important we were in her life to help her through that. Not even a year later—this happened in April and by that September, we dedicated a brand new pole and flag at the field for the brother. And we had the news come out and we had the [military] there. It was a hell of an event. Going from the worst part of it to a pre- and post-game ceremony, where they brought the flag down and folded it, and presented it to her. To see part of what an impact we can have on someone's life. And last year she ran in a marathon for him, so we went to it. Just anything else that you can do to be a part of their lives that's off the field. You get up that morning, you drive to watch her run in the marathon, the five seconds as she runs by, but that's what you do, so she'll always be a part of our lives.

Some coaches wanted to establish a relational environment for their players, but found themselves much less successful than Clara. Some women struggled with negative attitudes amongst players and with their own personal fears of how to build those relationships. Hannah, a D2 coach, spoke about how evaluating herself as a coach came down to more than just the team's win-loss record. She noted that her first few years were tough in the conference, often having mediocre results in games. Yet she didn't want to focus on just those criteria for herself as a good coach. There was more, and it involved social and behavioral benchmarks:

> For me as a coach, I want to see improvements in all areas that we talk about in the goals, and I want to feel like I'm having an impact on these kids, these players, individually. And I can't say with that senior class— it's the first group of players in my coaching career that I feel like I haven't been able to have an impact like I would have liked to. I don't feel like they got any better in their four years; I feel like some of them got worse.

One story she shared from a few years prior clearly showed the conflict of trying to influence the environment:

> The night before Senior Day—we have eleven seniors and we hadn't won a game in the conference. There's this tradition that I haven't upheld of starting all seniors on Senior Day—I had made a decision that I wasn't gonna start all the seniors. I communicated that to the team the night before, and that night in text messages, emails from parents, from the players was, "This is a disgrace, this is our last year, give us something. We can compete." So what do I do? I backed down.

> Before going onto the field, I brought in all the seniors and said, "Listen, this is what we're gonna do." And I gave them my expectations of them and kind of let it out—why I'd made the decision before hand. And there were some tears and frustrations. I also communicated

to them why I had made this decision, and how I feel there has been this lack of respect and here I am—and I said, "I'm gonna give you this opportunity, but I have these expectations of you." We go out and in the first 15 minutes, we're down 3-0 to this team who is in the bottom of the pack—and this team we're playing averaged one goal a game. So I start subbing the freshman in, and one of the fathers on the other side of the field yells, "Let the seniors play, Coach!" And we're 3-0, which is a big deficit in 15 minutes in soccer.

She noted, "You're either the bitch or too nice."

For these coaches, there is a mix of how to "do gender" and influence the kids. Some coaches just want to change the structure, while others focus on the individuals; for Hannah, it was a mix. Importantly, she felt little support from the administration (who she told me were present at the game but did nothing to support her). She was quick to note that most often her hardest struggle has been from the dads:

We have tailgates after our [college] away games, and they're so friendly with you until their daughter starts not playing. I had one dad at the tailgate—the tailgate was down this road, so I had to walk down this road—and the father stood there like this, with his arms crossed, just glaring at me. And my mom had come to the game with me, and I'm like, "Mom, that's one of the dads of a player that didn't play." And he just glared at me while I walked by. I walked my mom to the car and she's like, "I can't believe you have to deal with that." And there was another dad who just cornered me after games and would talk about soccer stuff and his daughter, and where she should be playing, that sort of thing. I thought it was important to interact with parents so they got to know who's leading their daughters and the team and whatnot, but I got to the point where I would take as long as I could to get to the tailgate, spend 5 quality minutes there, and then just get on the bus and let them interact. It becomes personal for the parents.

Hannah summed up her frustration with her latest cohort that just finished their four years:

So I evaluate myself on the impact that I'm making on the players individually, with all those other things short term, but also long term that they can look back and say, "Wow, that person really had an influence on my life." And I can't say that a majority of those seniors that are graduating can say that about me. So that's the frustrating part.

What is interesting about this coach—and was true for all the women I met—was that she was constantly doing self-evaluation. She commented, "It's just self-evaluation all the time, and figuring out or understanding what it is, and what I can do to make sure that doesn't happen again." Later she added, "Even if I didn't have the wins, if I felt like I was having an impact on those kids, it would be different."

When I first met Hannah, she was struggling with how some of her student-athletes didn't respect her or show her that respect. She was left feeling flummoxed and depressed:

And so there were things that happened during the last four years—where I didn't put a firm foot down early enough, and they just pushed and pushed and pushed. And instead of me setting the tone, I allowed them to kind of run the program. And it made me unhappy.

Hannah's story points to the bigger issue of how these coaches balance being tough and caring at the same time. It is interesting that some researchers argue women can't do or be both, but that is exactly what a good coach does.[27] Kathy, a D3 coach, said "I'm relational, these girls are my children, this is what I do, it's the way I go. So when you decide to engage fully in any given relationship, it's not gonna be easy because loving people well isn't easy, because lives are messy."

This notion of balancing being hard and kind, helpful and distant, close and yet not too close (much like teaching or parenting) is a tricky one for coaches. All the coaches I spoke with brought it up in some form or fashion. Hannah seemed to articulate it most clearly. She wanted to put down boundaries, but really wrestled with knowing how and where to do that. She wanted her athletes to feel close enough to come to her and therefore build bonds, but in the effort to do so, she often left them feeling like she was trying too hard. Hannah said she wanted to put down a firm foot, but sometimes that foot stamped out the love side of the equation, and thus she engaged in self-blame:

---

27 As an aside, in my interviews with younger middle school players, one girl said a great female coach was someone who was your friend and motivator. We joked in the focus group about the terms and came up with the term "frotivator" as the term for the best coach trait.

So my personality, my way, is kind of like nurturing, caretaking. So the discipline side of things for me, it doesn't allow the kids to be accountable, and I enabled this poor behavior for the last few years. I've had to make some pretty hard decisions. It's hard for me to discipline kids and I've had to do it, and I've found that it's been pretty effective with this group. But yeah, I think I needed to do more of that to earn their respect, and to make them accountable for their actions and that sort of thing.

Hannah talked vividly about how her male counterparts had three rules, but when she tried those with female athletes, it just didn't work the same. (Ironically, the three rules hadn't worked for her to the extent that she couldn't even remember what they were.) What is interesting is that she was trying to impose structural changes without recognizing her own agency (or lack thereof) in the process. Hannah believed she could change the girls just as her male counterparts seemed to be able to affect their male players. What is important to recognize is that some of the female coaches I met struggled and questioned themselves. One wonders what further research needs to be done on women and confidence in sport. Women in sport can be quite confident, yet what about times when they are not? How do we foster confidence despite both external and internal barriers? In turn, how does this translate to the younger generation? If, in fact, we keep telling girls in 2019 that there are no barriers when there are, in fact, barriers, what will become of that frustration they feel when they are hitting the wall? All of these coaches were successful athletes, often playing with boys at a very young age, often with their dads as the coaches, and with no female role models, so they saw themselves as equal to males. They knew they were girls, but felt they were just as good as the boys on the field. Their parents never told them they weren't good enough or strong enough, and so they played on. In many cases, their dads were coaches, who spurred them on to push and succeed as female soccer players. Yet my work shows that as they enter into professional environs later in their careers, some men aren't so willing to play fairly in this gendered game, causing women to question themselves and their worthiness in their head coaching roles.

PROFESSIONALISM AND LONG-TERM PERSONHOOD

Although I did not talk to most coaches about their own long-term goals, as we so often focused instead on life histories and how they reached this point in their careers, they were *very* focused on long-term goals for their players. These coaches are extremely cognizant that their players' actions affect more than just their four years in college. Katelyn, a D3 coach, articulated it succinctly:

> You have them for four years, maybe only two. And you're just trying to help them gain the empowerment of being a female and being able to do whatever job they're going to be doing. Because whatever personality they bring to the team is going to be the personality they bring to the team where they're working. So coaching has two sides. You're coaching soccer, but you're also coaching them for real life.

Mia, a D1 coach, said it this way:

> Empower these young females so that after four years, they feel confident. And I think that's a really important

word because like you said, they're finding their voice and you really gotta help them find that voice and be confident and prepared and successful so they can do whatever the heck they want. So whether they're a little bit shy or a little bit more outspoken, I want them to find their voice and I take responsibility for that when somebody comes to play for me. And I think that's hugely important.

Annie, a D2 coach, recognized that understanding our core selves was critical to grasping, and teaching, lifelong lessons on professionalism:

I think to be a good person, it doesn't necessarily mean you're mistake-free, because none of my kids are mistake-free—nor am I mistake-free. I think it's learning from your experiences; it's being respectful both to yourself—that's mentally, physically, and emotionally—and also to others. And I think it's having confidence. Obviously, I don't think that's something that women are taught straight away. You can be outspoken, you can be raising your hand all the time, you can be the one stepping up, standing tall. I think that, for me, a good person is just someone that pays attention to their surroundings and is self-aware, like, "Hey, I can be a little bit sassy right now," or "I need to keep my mouth shut and respect this person, even if maybe I disagree." I think there's a way to do disagreements and confrontations healthily. Obviously, nothing comes up roses between people all the time, so I think understanding how to communicate and how to interact with their teammates will thus help them interact wherever they go, whether it's military service or grad school or a career, they need to understand that human element.

Another coach, Sarah, who is married to a social scientist, said that she actively learns from him, and thus she is vividly engaged in what she calls "the mental side of the game" in actual classroom settings. She told me her focus is on how her players can "be successful outside in the real world. How can they take these traits and take them out to when they graduate?" Her focus on their personal lives and choices led her to develop a mentoring program.

> They had to find a mentor for themselves, in any area of life that they felt that they needed mentoring, and then they identified what they thought their strength was and how they could help someone else and mentor them. So that was our project. We do a project every year outside of soccer. I find a project for them to do.

This program speaks to the desire of the young women for more than tactical skills drills and shooting practice on the field. They seem to gravitate to, and yearn for, discourse around the mental game. She noted that a recent conversation had been a favorite for the women:

> First, I asked them to define leadership, and none of them could give me a definition of leadership. They gave me traits that leaders may have, that they've seen different personality traits in them, but they didn't actually know what a leader did or what it meant to be in a leadership role. So once I gave them kind of what

it meant, we worked it out. We talked about looking at a vision and how the leader kind of sets that vision for a group, and they work toward that vision through communication in all different areas, and it's that vision that they're working toward.

Sarah continued to explain that she exposed the athletes to transformational and transactional leadership:

Transactional [leadership] was an exchange. They would ask you to do something, and you would do something in return. That was kind of how they defined the transactional leadership. Transformational [leadership] was bettering yourself. And so [the question was], how can a person inspire you to better yourself and help you work toward that goal in an individual sense? So they saw it as a negative and positive, and once we kind of looked at it as leaders can be in both positions and be very successful leaders and very positive leaders. They thought that in business, being a transactional leader would work better than being a transformational leader. And in something like soccer or sport, they thought a transformational leader would be better.

Yet Sarah, like many of her peers, realized that such conversations are not a one-time effort; rather, they are but one small part of changing these girls' lives for the long term. She added:

Yeah, in practice yesterday, we kind of tied that into it. It was amazing to see them to start tying those leadership things into practice, where I could step back and watch them and say, "Okay, these are the things we talked about on Sunday. Can you add these back into your game now?" And so they were starting to play with that. And it was probably the best practice we've had all year, even in our fall season. And that's what I said to my husband when I got home. It was an awesome practice, it was nice to see it, and I know what they learned that Sunday wasn't everything that they got, but it's a piece of a puzzle, and it's a very important piece of the puzzle.

Mia, a D1 coach, also had a very important point about the need for preparing players for life after college. She recalled talking to her mentor, Emma, after her own personal soccer playing years ended, saying "You lose a sense of your identity, and—I've said it before—I think we need to have some kind of programming to transition seniors, because I think it's taken for granted how hard that transition can be." These coaches think long term for their players, all while focusing on their own daily issues of schedules, recruitment, travel plans, and player development.

What impressed me about these women is that they show up for their players every day in ways people might not expect. Most individuals think coaching happens on the field and in locker rooms, yet these women show that it goes much farther. One D2 coach, Clara, spoke passionately about her broader life impact on these young women:

I know from my friends who are coaching or friends who are trying to get coaches jobs and are usually beat out by the male that I have this opportunity to be that person for these kids, so I want to do it to the best of my ability, but I also want them to enjoy it. I don't want them to leave here going, "Oh, we had a female coach and she was a pain in the butt." They get one shot at this for four years and I want it to be the best four years they can have.

I was left with a lasting impression of Clara and her massive role in young women's lives when she told the following story:

I had one of my players who went into the [military]. Her background was in graphic design, but she went in to do computer intelligence. So she went through training school, and at every training school, every group that goes through the training school gets to have their own badge or logo. She was allowed to design it for her squadron because of her background in graphic design, and she got given five of them to send to the five most important people who helped her get where she is, and I got one of those in the mail! So that type of pride, too. It's beyond here, it's following these kids for the next 30 years of their career. Knowing that she had an opportunity to send just five of these out, and you made the cut, type of thing.

What the vignette doesn't tell you is that she only confided in three people that she had even received the badge: her mother, her husband, and me! This is a woman who doesn't rest on her laurels, her accomplishments, and her ability. She quietly and privately keeps making huge differences in young women's lives. These coaches are impacting young athletes' college and future lives, in both tangible and intangible ways.

The critical final piece here is that outsiders, non-soccer people, parents, and even friends do not see or know how hard it is to coach. These female coaches do remarkable work, and yet people see it as easy or "just sports." Kathy, a D2 coach, said:

> One of my biggest struggles is being able to shut it all off at the end of the day. I'm not a parent, but I feel like I get a taste of that, and for me, personally, there's not a day that goes by—even in the summer now they're all gone—that I'm not concerned about someone, or things like that. I feel like, especially for female coaches and their desire to nurture their athletes more, I think it can be really hard on them mentally. And I think that's a real struggle for them that is not really identified, because again, people think we just play for a living.

Emma, a D1 coach, echoed a similar sentiment:

> I think they might not know the challenge of juggling family and a job. I don't think they know how emotional it can be to manage a team. It's not the Xs and Os that take the toll, that takes the energy. It's more the emotional piece of it, and just trying to do right, be right. And manage. Manage people, men or women. Manage kids. They might not know how difficult it is—it's not the part about being unappreciated by the student-athletes or challenged by the student-athletes. It's the outside forces that can just wear you down to the point where it's just not worth it. The parents—maybe in some cases, not in mine—the administration, the battles you have to fight to prove the importance of athletics, and athletics for women.

Later at the end of our interview she says, "Women don't tend to be Teflon, they take in the feedback and take it to heart." Certainly the female coaches I met take their jobs to heart—they care, they want to do the right thing, and they want to be a hugely positive influence on younger women.

CONCLUSIONS

Most outsiders to the world of soccer—passing by precisely manicured fields, scoreboards, and media booths—have no idea that our coaches are engaging in such remarkable character building at the micro level for both their players and themselves. Most outsiders to the soccer world do not understand or see that female soccer coaches feel their jobs, as minorities in their occupations, are in fact a calling. The coaches I've met take their jobs so seriously—as I'm sure many male coaches do—but my research emphasizes that women tend to focus on making things right and making changes in soccer environs across the country. Coaching changes these young athletes and, in turn, changes the adult coaches as well.

Coaches don't coach in a vacuum; rather, their personality traits and levels of human agency affect the environments they work in. This complex mix of agency and structural constraint shapes their experience, attitudes, and beliefs about gender and soccer. They end up "doing gender" by using unique ways of influencing behavior, relational outlooks, and professionalism within their player base. Such influences are developed based upon their own personality traits and the structural boundaries of their athletic environments. If more coaches who happen to be women could speak out about their environs—and have those voices heard—we might be able to map out larger, more complete frameworks of gender and soccer. Although not surprising, what is new and unique about these data are the intimate details and struggles that become evident from these voices that have been hidden for so long. This research exposes the often unspoken intricacies of coaching, the components of the gender divide. In many ways my work dovetails quite nicely with that of Bernice Sandler and her work on microinequities and the chilly climate women face in certain environs. The irony is not lost on me that it has been 36 years since Hall and Sandler first published on the chilly climate and women are still fighting to get their voices heard. Thankfully these coaches are making headway in the gender fight.

Chapter 6

Not Just Doing Coaching But Surviving Coaching: Strategies Coaches Use in the Workplace

Women who eventually become first-time head coaches often find themselves in unfamiliar surroundings with little prior knowledge of how to navigate their new responsibilities. It is not that they don't know how to play soccer or that they aren't good at coaching, but they have never been in collegiate work environments sitting at the head coach's desk. Although a handful of them did end up as head coaches at institutions they attended as undergraduate students or where they had been an assistant coach, it was a different scenario when the entire team outlook and trajectory was upon their shoulders. The view of the team probably looked very different from the other side of the coaching desk. In addition, many of them looked around and saw very few women in the hallways and conference rooms of their respective athletic departments. Thus, they found themselves in a unique situation: well trained and professionally poised to begin their head coaching careers, yet faced with a lot of responsibility with little knowledge of how to get things done, and few female colleagues within their athletic departments. My research shows that women consequently engage in four main strategies for navigating their new terrain:

- attempting to create new allies within their athletic departments;

- relying upon male mentors (often male coaches from earlier in their career arc);

- fighting back against the sexism; and

- finally, in a very few cases, retreating or quitting.

MEN, MENTORING, AND QUEEN BEES

Looking for male mentors in the workplace is not unique to the soccer world. In fact, a large segment of the gender and business literature today shows that women who reach the top echelons of their fields and who have few female counterparts, often "approach men for mentor relationships" (Vincent & Seymour, p. 5). Yet beyond what initially appears to be benign positioning, these authors show that women at the top often feel the need to protect their own career arcs and successes instead of helping in the advancement of other women. Thus, senior women hold on to their positions tightly, distancing themselves from women in the lower ranks. This phenomenon is known as the Queen Bee Syndrome (QBS) whereby "women leaders in organizations in which most executive positions are held by men may reproduce rather than challenge the existing gender hierarchy" (Derks, Van Laar, Ellemers, & de Groot, 2015, p. 456). It appears that the QBS seems tightly linked to women's isolated positions at the top of corporations. In response, these female workers turn to male colleagues in the top echelons for help, guidance, and aid. Such males are better positioned within companies to offer career support due to their greater knowledge and power within the company (Lockwood, 37). In some cases, senior-level women actually don't want to mentor younger women because the appearance is one of a female power coalition and they know that won't fare well in the workplace dynamics for their personal advancement (Vincent & Seymour, 5). Thus, their queen bee actions solidify their respective positions, allowing them greater control over an often-tenuous workplace, all while alienating younger women.

The majority of coaches spoke of often being one of "few women in the room or at the table." Such findings resonate with the work of Sheryl Sandberg (2013, p. 9). Sandberg argues that women often "act like spectators rather than participants" in business meetings, given the gender hierarchy in the room (p. 29). Thus, she encourages women to strive ahead, find and utilize the many ways to the top, and to always take risks. The coaches I met were doing just that.

In many ways, these coaches were renegades who, like their business counterparts, "climbed and kicked" to get there (see Kaiser 2015, p. 600). Kaiser notes that women in these top corporate positions "who are most capable of advancing in domains in which their group is underrepresented are those who value self-promotion and advancement over group-level advancement and are therefore unlikely to advocate on behalf of other group members" (p. 600). Yet nothing could be farther from the truth about the female coaches I met. These coaches strive to guide and mentor younger female players to succeed in soccer (see previous chapter), akin to what Vincent and Seymour call a "multiplying effect" (1995, p. 10). Thus, these female mentors become critical for other women in the workplace (Lockwood, p. 44). One wonders if, and how, sport engenders a certain environment to make women want to help other women, as opposed to distancing themselves from one another.

In business then, given the propensity for QBS actions, corporate women typically turn to men for help within the workplace, a phenomenon called cross-gender mentoring. Vincent and Seymour argue such mentoring gives women "personal and career development, career rejuvenation, advancement, peer recognition, and a loyal base of support" (p. 9).

Similarly, the majority of female coaches I met had few close female mentors within the top levels of their current athletic departments and so, like their female business counterparts, often turned to male mentors. But what is different is that they often looked beyond their departments to find male mentors from their own personal history—and they don't engage in the Queen Bee scenario. Thus, the coaches ended up engaging in cross-gender mentoring that was also long-distance mentoring. These mentors—although often hundreds of miles away—offered planning, emotional, and procedural types of support. These three levels of investment were critical for my respondents' sense of overall well-being and rootedness. I found that the main reasons they turned to their mentor were for job opportunities, a loyal support base, and job performance advice. My findings are valuable, as they explore how long distance mentoring impacts women's lives, but they also raise the idea of how such e-mentoring, as it often called today, might help many women in other fields who lack female or male mentors within close proximity in their companies or organizations.

MALE MENTORS: OFFERING CAREER PLANNING, EMOTIONAL, AND PROCEDURAL SUPPORT

CAREER PLANNING SUPPORT

Often the male mentors strongly influenced the female coaches' career decisions long before the women became head coaches. Clearly this social influence involved emotional support, which I will turn to later in this chapter, but initially the mentors gave advice about job openings and career opportunities. These men were the women's first undergraduate coaches or the head coaches they worked for when they took their first assistant coaching jobs. It was often the mentor who contacted the protégé and said, "Hey, this job is opening, you should apply." Several women talked about how such opportunities simply fell upon them, due to those relationships. It is clear that these men had broad knowledge of the soccer world, opportunities, and shifts in hiring and firing. These bits of information then become direct conduits to job vacancies for many women I met.

Melanie got an assistant coach job at a DI school, but unfortunately found herself in an environment of disorganization and didn't feel connected to the coach or players. She decided to leave when a former male mentor (her D3 assistant coach from when she was an undergrad) told her to get out of that job, as people were starting to associate her with the negative facets of the D1 coach and program. Her male mentor told her that if she didn't leave the D1 job, her name "was gonna be mud." She eventually ended up as a head coach at a D3 school and has happily been there for the past ten years. Such stories provide evidence, as mentioned earlier, of the small, tight circles within the collegiate soccer world.

Mia, a D1 coach, also had a valuable male mentor, who was her AD in her first assistant coaching job. She told me about how she had been nervous to take a new head coaching job, but recalled how this male mentor encouraged her to step out and conquer her fear. He told her:

> "Mia, sometimes you have to go away in order to come back." And it kind of stuck with me, because I was scared about going to [a different university] where I didn't know anyone. That was scary for me. So that really boosted me and gave me a lot of confidence. And when I got hired back, I felt he was delighted to have me back, and then when it was time to go, he was the same thing.

Additionally, these mentors gave guidance as the women took on their first assistant coach or head coaching jobs. As Humberd and Rouse (2016) point out, "through observational learning, proteges model the behaviors and activities of their mentors and identify with them, viewing the mentors as models of who they want to become in the future" (p. 435). What is most significant for the female coaches is that while a power differential and hierarchy once structured these mentoring relationships, these later evolve into warm, almost familial relationships. Sandberg (2013) notes that mentoring relationships can turn into friendships, but that the "foundation is a professional relationship" (p. 67). She also points out that males in most work mentoring situations want to mentor younger men (p. 70), but clearly in the soccer world these older males were genuinely interested in mentoring younger women who they thought had talent and great potential. Such findings point to the intricate nature of gender relations, and to gender collaboration in places where we might not expect to find it. Here again I am struck by the unique components of sport in these women's lives: competition and inequality in the midst of mentoring, positive relationships, and collaboration.

EMOTIONAL SUPPORT: MALES WHO ARE GENDER AWARE

Most female coaches met their male mentors early in their careers, often playing for them as an undergraduate player, or working under them as an assistant in their first professional jobs. They often spoke of those early days as ones of uncertainty and tenuous personal and professional development. Luckily, they had good male mentors to rely upon for emotional support and friendship. Clara, a D2 head coach, developed a strong relationship with four male mentors, but spoke passionately about the care and compassion of her first undergrad coach when she blew out her ACL and MCL on the first day of preseason. Being an international student, she was far away from home and her new coach's actions made a huge impression upon her and her parents.

> He didn't even recruit us. We were recruited by the coach prior to him and that coach was fired during the summer. He was [from the UK], he had moved away from home. He had a very nurturing sense to me, a very, very caring guy. I think he knew that if I left and went back to

England, I wasn't gonna get the rehab I was gonna [need] and I probably wouldn't have recovered from this the way I did out here. And he basically did everything to make sure I wasn't gonna leave, either. And I think, instantly, my mum could see that. They moved me off campus just because I was in a dorm that, at the time, didn't have an elevator, so I actually moved into what they considered the soccer house, and my mum moved in too, so they turned their little room into a spare bedroom for my mum and I. So my mum's seeing the kids do this, seeing Joe visit with me every day, even on the days I couldn't get to school. My mum's an intelligent person and she could see—she said the hardest thing for her was me being away from home, but she also knew it was the best thing for me.

Clara talked about the impact his personality and character made on her:

I guess it just comes down to the type of guy he is. He still is one of my first phone calls now whenever I have good news, bad news, he's the first person I call. That's just the type of person he was and the relationship that developed over the years.

Erin, a D3 coach, spoke similarly about an early college coach who cared about who she was as a human being. Erin was a mother and coach who spoke passionately about wanting to see more women in coaching roles.[28] Erin has also wanted that for young female

---

28   A top national female administrator shared a similar sentiment, when she noted in our conversation that today for female athletes, "if you can see it, you can be it." She argued most women, though, don't go into coaching because they have few role models and often don't think of coaching as a viable option.

athletes. I believe that much of her passion regarding gender and athletics comes from this notion of being seen. I think in many ways she was influenced heavily by her second college coach who exemplified the mentality of coaching the whole player:

> Just about how you get better. Like, "Hey Erin, you played really well yesterday. You did this, but you're still diving in," or "You need to make better passes out of the back." He would just be more specific and say, "Hey, here's what you need to work on." He was tough. He cared and he wanted to help people get better, but he didn't let you slack off. For the first time, I had a coach—male or anyone really—that could do both sides of it. He cared about me as a person and wanted me to succeed, but he wanted to push me, he had to give me the tools. So that was the first time that I had ever really had that, honestly. And obviously it made a big impact on me. He was great. He changed the program, too. It had already been successful but there's no way we would have gone to the final four if we hadn't had him. I'm very certain of that.

Melanie, a D3 coach, spoke about how her male mentors were gender aware males that gave her balance, centeredness, and stability, so that she could find her own confidence:

> I had this incredible—my coach was a male and he was incredibly intense and really demanded a lot of you, and for many of my teammates, that did not resonate with them and they really didn't like him. It really worked for me, because I read it as, "Oh my God, he believes in me more than I believe in me." And he pulled me to places I wouldn't have gone. Now were his methods

great all the time? Probably not, and I don't necessarily use them, but I still to this day have a fantastic relationship with him.

Later in our interview, Melanie shared how that relationship still nurtures her:

I had an assistant coach who left after two years. And I would say he and I were pretty close, but my relationship with my head coach continued. And to this day, his life has taken some funky turns and I think our relationship has really turned into a friendship, and it's really cool. I would actually call us friends now.

She went on to reveal how her personal life and athletic life collided (with positive repercussions):

I was one of those people—and I still am—someone that is just relationship oriented and very small-group oriented. I like to call myself a high-energy introvert. But I was the player that stopped by their office all the time, and so I created these relationships with them, mostly based on humor, and then what happened in college, real life hit. I lost a friend to suicide and then I really got close to them.

She developed a similarly close relationship when she secured her first job as a D3 assistant coach. She talked about another male mentor in her past who was gender aware:

And I had a great—I mean, I got so lucky. And I credit my boss there, and he's still the head women's coach there. I had such a good experience with him. He's the reason I'm in coaching. Because I have some of my friends that, if you don't get a good boss, they get out, and he was so wonderful. I think he really respects the women's game. His wife actually was a coach at [college x] for 12 years, so their family's even instrumental in me being here. He has a lot of respect for his players, he has a lot of respect just for women in general. There was no difference, it wasn't slumming to be with the women's team. I think sometimes you get the vibe from people that they are in this profession because they couldn't get—it's just a holding place, until they can get into a higher level, be it Division 1 or be it the men's game, or something like that. And [he] did not, he's not like that. Soccer is soccer to him. And he's just—I call him a very evolved, self-aware man.

She went on to say, "And I think he really was invested in my path. I think he saw an ability in me that I didn't know I had." When I asked her why she thought he was so evolved as a male, our conversation took a vast divergent turn. Melanie referenced Christine Brennan's book *Best Seat in the House* (2006), noting that the "whole premise in her work is that behind every powerful woman is a man, who like put you there." I tell her ironically that I see that in much of my data and she replies that "it is a feminist message, because men should be feminists." Her comments raise interesting questions about gender, mentoring, culture, and identity. Who significantly shapes our gender identity as women in sport? What values do they try to instill in us as women, and why? Why are some men engaged in lip service advocacy while others care about true gender advocacy?

How do we get more fathers to be gender-aware males for their daughters?[29]

Some women actually talked about their mentors as being like family. Margaret, a D3 coach, talks of her first mentor—her undergraduate coach—as a second dad, and noted that they remain close friends today. They had a good relationship, with Margaret initially seeing his office as a place where she could talk about games, life, and college:

> He was at a point where he was feeling burned out and just didn't feel like players cared. So having me—I'm not saying it was just me, but having a group of us always in his office—helped light a fire under his butt a little bit. And we just had a really good relationship. The joke was, when he was recruiting me, that the south never gets snow. First year I was there, they got 5 feet of snow. And I couldn't go home for Christmas, my flight got canceled, so I ended up going home with friends, and we were texting the whole time. I was like, "I'm transferring, you lied!" You know, we're joking around. And I've just always had that really good relationship. And then when I started maturing through college and hit my junior year, it was the last day to change your major for that year, and I went to his office. I'm in tears, because I'm like, "I'm gonna have to be here for another year, what am I going to do?

---

29 Melanie and several others had fathers that created paths for their soccer dreams early on. Sydney, for example, spoke of being on the family team, while Melanie credits her father for saving her soccer career; after she and her misfit friends, as she puts it, didn't make the local rec team, her father created his own team. As an aside, one wonders again (see earlier chapter on hyper-invested fathers), if this helped or hindered these women in particular ways. More research needs to focus on the influence of gender-aware men.

I'm gonna have to take two classes as a fifth-year senior." Oh my gosh, and I didn't even go to my parents, he was the first person I went to. And he really pushed me— Oh great, I don't know why I'm crying, I'm so sorry.

She continued to speak about how her parents were 10 hours away, but her coach instilled confidence and support in her. Margaret's experience seems to reflect the notion by Feist-Price (1994) that "more often than not, mentoring relationships parallel parenting relationships due to such patterns as authority, respect, intimacy and trust" (p. 13). Margaret continued:

So my soccer coach was the only one that I could go to and be like, "I have so much on my plate right now, what do I do?" And my lacrosse coach, she was very much like a second mom. But my soccer coach's office was closer to campus so I always ended up being there. Both of them together kind of helped me push to it, but he was like, "Margaret, you're a great player. Why would you not be a college coach? You don't like any of the other majors. Every time you talk about what you want to do post college, you talk about coaching. Let's do this." So my senior year, I interned with him, and just kind of helped out more with recruiting, got a good feel for that. We talked a lot about compliance, he made sure I read the rule books so I understood what was going on. And I think he didn't want to tell me right off the bat that I was going to coach with him next year. I think he was kind of holding me in this loop, saying I'm gonna volunteer. But he ended up not posting the job and saying, "No, I really want to bring you on," and we had a great relationship to begin with, but we had an even better one after. He and I talk a lot. I talked to him yesterday for like an hour. He's just very much a predominant figure in my coaching career and he helped me understand the game. I thought I knew the game, like any player does, but then you get on the other side of it and really see it. And together, we had one of the best recruiting classes for soccer in quite some time, and then they ended up making playoffs. So it was really great. And he used—or abused—the privilege of sending me on the road, because I don't have a family. So he'd be like, "Hey, what are you doing this weekend?" I'd be like, "Oh, nothing." He'd say, "Great, you're going to Chico. There's a bunch of games going on, here's the schedule, go see so and so and so and so. Get it done." So we just had a really good relationship like that.

In some cases, it was a male athletic director who gave emotional support and job advice. Annie, a D2 coach, recalled her early days in her first head coaching job:

My athletic director, who was also a male, was one of the best people I've ever worked for in my life, and I can't say more about that man. He is retiring, this is his last year. He's been at the same university for almost 40 years, I think. I love him and he's a hard ass, tells it like it is, very honest. Ruffled feathers, I think, but he was like a dad to me. I could go in his office and just chat, like, "I'm not making enough money, can you help me out?" And he was always so honest and did a lot to keep me there.

Later she mentioned that this AD had moved to the southeastern part of the U.S., and she and her husband were going to visit him soon after our interview took place, noting that he was "just an awesome guy, really real, and his big thing is everything he does is for the student-athletes, and I really respect that."

Sometimes mentors not only gave emotional support, but also gave specific organizational information, knowledge, or advice. Later in our interview, Annie was reminded of another male mentor earlier in her career arc who taught her how to navigate departmental procedures:

> He was great. He was so supportive, I think in addition to my coach here, he was another role model. Very, very different, very quiet. Funny—I mean he wouldn't be that way around the players, but very funny with me. His sense of humor was great. But not as expressive as my coach here, who was literally blue in the face, screaming on the sidelines. [His] style was arms crossed, more of an observer, and a fixer at halftime. But we would sit in the office together all day. We shared an office because there really wasn't a space for me. We spent a lot of time together, we'd go get lunch. He has two daughters who are obviously a lot younger than me, but he was a good guy, saying, "Annie you want this, you want that?" Giving me things that would help me kind of grow, even some paperwork stuff, because no one ever tells you all the paperwork and administrative stuff that goes along with coaching, but he would give me little tasks there to help me learn that stuff, and it was definitely a good kind of teaching relationship.

What these female coaches kept coming back to was that having these male mentors believe in them and encourage them cemented some sort of belief and strength inside themselves. One D1 coach I met, when asked who mentored and encouraged her, recounted the three specific men in her hometown who believed so strongly in girls at a young age that they had built sporting teams for them in an age, and town, where few female teams existed at the time:

> Oh my God, I remember those three guys. They were our coaches all the way through our youth. I went to Stew's funeral a few years ago, and Mr. Bailey passed away, too. I'm not actually sure what happened to Mr. Smith. But I went to Stew Clarkson's funeral because he was so significant to my childhood, my opportunity to play—all three of them were. I'll never forget them.

One wonders what significance gender made in this soccer development equation. If it had been a woman, would those relationships have felt as powerful? The answer is probably yes, but might the relationships have been different, and how? Or did cross-gender mentoring offer the women something psychologically beyond just guidance? To put this a different way, did having a male soccer coach believe in them and value them mean more than having a female coach? Do such positive, cross-gendered relationships lend validity and worth to women in male-dominated spaces that often ignore women? Such questions are critical for workplace analyses today, as research shows that women are less confident in certain spaces than men (see Niraj Chokshi, 2018). If, in fact, women are hesitant to speak up or recognize their own abilities in biology classrooms[30]—where

---

30 Such findings resonate closely with Hall and Sandler's 1982 work on the chilly climate in which patterns of verbal and non-verbal behavior by teachers made girls uncomfortable and hesitant to speak up in comparison to their male counterparts who commanded the teacher's attention (p.7).

Chokshi notes their numbers exceed that of male students—might they be less able to speak up in soccer environs where they are fully outnumbered by males? How do positive male influences change those feelings for women and men? Could cross-gender mentoring increase women's agency in soccer environs where there are few female colleagues? Such scenarios might have broader implications for women in other isolated fields across the world. In addition, more research needs to explore what such cross-gender mentoring relationships give to men.

LOOKING FOR ALLIES

Another strategy that coaches used in the workplace was focusing internally and attempting to make allies, male or female. Yet the environs they found themselves in were most definitely a chilly climate for women, steeped in a history of male-dominated views and perspectives (see previous chapter). It is intriguing that the majority of the D2 and D3 coaches had played with boys at a young age in neighborhood pick-up games and even in their early rec and club soccer days. Yet, despite their confidence, abilities, and skills, it was often adult males that had problems with talented athletic girls, not their younger male peers. Erin, a D3 coach, remembered a lesson from when she was in elementary school, the memories etched into her mind decades later:

> I actually tell my team about this every once in a while. When I was really young—this was co-ed, I was probably 5 or 6—I matured a little faster than the boys, so I was faster than most of the boys, I was pretty tough. We had a practice one day where there was a track around the field we were playing on and the coach said,

"All right, we're gonna do a little bit of running. The first three people that win are gonna get a pack of Juicy Fruit gum." So I was like, "Heck yeah! Competition, I'm in." So I take off, we do our two laps, I smoked everybody. And we get back in there and he wouldn't give me the pack of gum. He said I cheated, he said I cut the course, which I didn't. He gave it to three boys. So I was upset, I was confused, I was frustrated. I was probably six. And my mom—I give her so much credit for this because she kind of kept her tongue—when we got to the car, started asking me how I felt. She's like, "I'm really sorry that happened." I was saying, "It's not fair, I don't understand." And she said to me, "Erin, the gum is the least important part of this. The important thing is that you know that you did it right. You can't control what he did. I can buy you a pack of gum to learn that you always do things the right way, and that's just the way you do it." So my mom, who doesn't really know much about sports, was amazing.

Sydney, a D2 coach, moved beyond the concept of fairness in our interview to note that boys and girls simply were encouraged in the world in different ways. She felt such socialization affected her role within coaching:

My feeling on it is that we raise our boys to feel that if they want something, they deserve it. But we raise our women to believe that if you really want something, there's a reason you probably shouldn't have it. There's like shame that goes with desire. So I think that translates into how they perform. Men, you have to convince that they're human and they make mistakes, and women, we spend most of our time telling you you're actually doing a really good job, because they're so hyper-aware of mistakes—and even things that aren't mistakes. So it's just a completely different philosophy. I'm not saying they're insecure, I'm not having to build them up, but they're so much more critical of themselves than I see in their male counterparts.

Hannah recounted how, even at the club level, the male coaches did not fully understand the girls:

I remember one coach would always talk about how the girls needed to play like boys. And that was actually from the director of the club. He would talk to the girls—he coaches some of the younger teams—and he would talk to the girls about going to battle and talk to them about needing to play like boys. And I would always confront him and talk to him about how we want our girls to play like girls. Different than playing like a boy. So I was fighting that all the time. And other things that—one of the males swore a lot, up and down the sidelines [at his girls' team]. Just the way he spoke to the team, in a degrading way.

This brings to mind Dan Blank's 2014 book entitled *Everything Your Coach Never Told You Because You're a Girl: and Other Truths About Winning*. In it he argues (unfortunately) that girls will only win and be successful if they play like they are boys. They need to leave behind the makeup, drama, and emotions, and simply play like male athletes. He argues that only then will they win. Ironically, all of the endorsements on the back cover were from male soccer coaches. I didn't see one female name saying "Yes, let's play exactly like boys."

Other women encountered male colleagues who believed in coaching males and females differently. Katelyn summed up a female versus male mentality of coaching:

> Women coaches would prevail because we're more about finesse. We're more about working together and getting it done. I think in the male coach's mind, they're interpreting the game as the technical part of it: "What do you mean, you can't pass? You should already know how to pass." As a female coach, I've always taken it and broken it down to the beginning again. Even though I know you know how to play, I want you to know how I want you to play. I don't think male coaches do that. So they'll yell more to get you to do what they want: "What do you mean, you can't pass? You were supposed to pass to so-and-so over there." But the male coaches are only basing their knowledge on what they know and can see. We're basing it on breaking it down and building it back up.

When asked to elaborate, she said this:

> Not breaking the athlete down, but breaking their skills down. Pretty much like I said, my first day of practice is about going back to the basics. I'm gonna teach you the basics because I'm gonna make sure that you know how I want them done. And if you don't know how to do them, we're gonna teach you how to do them, and I'm not gonna yell at you for something that you don't know

or that I haven't coached you on. The teamwork that goes on in a women's game is so much different than a men's game. In a female's game, you're seeing teams work together. In a male's game, you *may* see a team sort of work together, but you're also going to start to see individuals work. By themselves. Because in a male soccer game, they're only about themselves.

When asked "What are women about?" she replied:

The team. That's the main goal. What is the goal of the team? You can go around and have individual goals, you can have your individual goal as a player, but what's the team goal? And is it realistic and can we meet that goal? If we say, "Yes, that's our goal." If you say no, if one person doubts that goal, then we're gonna change the goal. And so I think it's a lot of that. And I don't think the men—I've never seen a male team get together and be like, "What is our team goal today? What are we doing today?"

At the end of my conversation with Katelyn, I asked her what she wanted people to know about female coaches. She said, "We have the ability to do the same thing, we have the same knowledge as a male coach. Soccer is soccer, it doesn't change. It's not like learning French and Spanish."

One D1 coach, Mia, spoke strongly, though, about a slightly different problem for female coaches which is that some men want to coach women because they think it's less competitive, and thus easier. Such comments came up from a few of the coaches that I met. Mia said:

This is one of the biggest issues right now in our industry: male soccer coaches coaching female college teams. That's an area that absolutely drives me crazy because I've heard this said—they think they can't cut it on the men's side because it's too competitive, and they think they can coach women because it's an easier opportunity for them to get. And without having experience in it, without having the understanding, they're getting jobs, in my opinion, not because they're more qualified but maybe they come in and they're more confident, maybe they've fudged a little bit of their resume. Maybe they have their buddy call the AD. I don't exactly know the root of it, but I find that to be one of the most infuriating things. I really try to be an advocate to promote female coaches, I think it's a wonderful thing. Again, not that it has to be a female that coaches a female, but it should be said that they understand the dynamics of how to get the best out of their athletes. And the fact that it's just, "Oh, it's an easier job to get," or "The men's side is too competitive, I'll just come to the girls' side, even though I don't know how to properly coach females or haven't had the experience," I just find that to be absolutely ridiculous.

She went on to tell me about a recent D1 women's team head coach position that was given to a male:

And it was disgusting, because the conversations I've heard this man have, he has no desire to even be on the women's team, he took the job to make extra money because he was getting married that year. So what I found disgusting and it just beyond frustrates me, is that he doesn't even have a desire, but just gets tossed this job.

Sydney, a D2 coach, even mentioned to me that she knew some men who had been given head coaching jobs for women's teams, even though they had never played collegiate soccer. We discussed how such opportunities were akin to her applying to coach a male collegiate basketball team, which we both agreed simply would not happen. In my conversation with Mia, we talked about a similar fictional scenario and I stated that if a woman applied for a job with no background in that sport, "They'd laugh you out of the room." Mia responded, "I'd want them to, because it's wrong!"

Some coaches, like Sarah, looked around, compared herself to the present male coach where she works, and commented that they are nothing alike. She noted that he is verbally abusive, often swearing at his team, telling them to "put away their fucking purses," and "take off their skirts." She told me that his female athletic trainer eventually moved over to work with Sarah's female team, as she couldn't handle his sexism. This young trainer had reached out to the male ADs on campus for support, but got no response, as they told her "that was just his style of coaching." Such data raises questions about what we expect from females versus what we expect from males, and how we conceptualize their respective attitudes and behaviors.

Yet beyond intrinsic differences in how the world sees girls and boys, female coaches wanted to find male allies that would support their coaching work. Some women I met did find some of their male colleagues to be extremely helpful. Kathy, a D2 coach, described a difficult situation with a student who broke strict campus rules about drinking at her conservative faith-based institution. Kathy dissolved the student's scholarship and cut her from the team, which greatly angered the student's parents. At the time, Kathy found huge support from a male colleague, the women's head basketball coach at her institution:

> I looked up to [him] because for me, when I need to make the right decisions, sometimes it takes me a little bit of time. [His] ability to make the right decision immediately is unparalleled. This guy is just a true guy of real character. So I purposefully went to the office early so I could see him. Still to this day, he and I sit and talk out team issues and work through them together. It's now become kind of a two-way street. We share books that won't always have to do with our sport, but have to do with our job. If I've read a really good book that I think he should read, I'll pass it on to him and vice versa. So I went into the office early the next day and I told him what I was doing, and he stood behind me 100%. Emails came from other parents who weren't even involved, who were upset with me about it, and stuff like that.

Hannah, a D2 coach, also relies upon her male colleagues for two reasons: They are often the only other soccer coaches there, and she feels their male perspective holds merit and valuable truths.

> They're more black and white, which is helpful for me, because I'm lots of gray. So that, I've found, has been helpful for me, because the emotional piece comes into it and then I can get clouded with judgment, sometimes because the emotions come into it, so it's been helpful

to communicate with some of my male coaching peers. They can give you perspective in a different way, without the emotions. And with the male coaches, it's just the Xs and Os, the black and white. Yeah, it's definitely different, I never really thought of it that way. And I find myself gravitating toward getting feedback from the males, because I think, for me, I already have all that emotional stuff and it's sometimes too much, so I seek those guys out just to be like, all right.

Yet, the women sometimes encounter male colleagues who don't process coaching pedagogy in a similar fashion. Hannah remembers when she cut an athlete, and as she put it "I got my first 'F-you' in an email!" Frustrated and upset, Hannah talked to her male counterpart about the experience. His response was the complete polar opposite of what she had faced. He told her, "I bring them in, I talk to them, and that's the end of it." For Hannah, the road was not so smooth. "For me, I bring the kid in, have the conversation, the parents get involved, there are phone calls calling me out on my decision making, that sort of thing." Again, gender variance plays a pivotal role in these parental responses, and in many ways relates to the gender microaggressions the female athletes face (see chapter 4).

It seems that male coaches were able to move on, let go, and not get embedded in such issues. Hannah recounts her male officemate's take on winning and losing (he coaches another varsity male sport which is not soccer):

We're so different, like he sees how I interact with my players and how I function as a coach. We're really different but it's kind of cool to see the differences. The other day, I was at their game and they were up most of the game, and they lost right at the end. I think for men—and I could be totally wrong—they lose, and it's like, "Okay, get to work. How can we win the next game?" Where women, like myself, will kind of dwell on, "What did we do wrong, and what went wrong?" The men's soccer coach has a saying: "Moving forward, moving forward" or whatever. And they lost and the next day, they were in doing film, watching for the next game. So instead of hashing out what went wrong or mistakes maybe that have been made, it's like, "Okay, done with that one, let's move on." Whereas someone like myself, female, I'm hashing every second of the game. Can't sleep.

I commented in response that yes, maybe women dwell and men don't. Hannah responded brusquely:

Is there a better word than *dwell*? *Dwell* seems so negative. You want to work hard to correct, even though you can't make those changes. Like it's a different perspective from fixing it to moving forward.

Coaches like Hannah were quick to try and avoid looking negative or overly sensitive. They struggled to want to have less emotional turmoil, like men, while really not being like their male counterparts at all. Such an ongoing struggle was never easy.

In some cases, the female coaches also find it harder to earn respect within the campus community. Hannah felt that men were automatically given respect, while women had to earn that.

(I should note one male colleague on campus calls her "the nice coach," because she is so nurturing.) In addition, in a former job, her male counterpart said watching women's soccer was like "watching a turtle walk." She relayed:

> Another example I have for that is when I was a young coach, probably in my 20s at the time, coaching a club team. Maybe it was an Olympic Development team, but I remember we had a session and I had brought in [my male assistant] at the time. And he's just a little bit younger than me. I had been coaching this team for weeks, and I just brought him in as my assistant. And I'm like, "John let's have you run the session tomorrow." And when the team showed up, there was this aura of respect for him. Like I had to earn my respect over time, but they like, listened, eye contact, you name it. And even now sometimes, when I talk to my players, they're a little less attentive than when—like sometimes I'll ask one of my [male] assistants to run a training session, and they get on it. The players get on it when the male is speaking. And for me—I feel for females—you have to earn that over time. For males, it's like, you have that respect and you can lose it, but for females, you've already lost it and you have to gain it.

Ironically, she added that she had coached boys' teams, and they were very respectful of her. She commented on another female coach she knows who coaches male high school boys. Hannah argued that, "to her face they are very respectful, versus like the women, I feel for me, have not been respectful to my face." So, what is it that we are teaching girls about respect at a young age that is different? This is a really troubling question, and the answer is equally troubling. Girls are being told that they can do anything, anywhere, any place, and yet find out the structural constraints of the world are not that easy. One wonders if females subconsciously want to please male coaches more, much like the Queen Bee analysis, as they know men hold the power within the environment.

Some women I met sounded quite lonely without female support. Hannah, who had two male assistants during the year I interviewed her, said:

> They have their strengths in a different way, which are really helpful, but my first year here I had three female assistant coaches. It was awesome, but definitely a lot of emotions. I definitely value having a little different perspective, but I definitely miss having at least one other female assistant coach. Sometimes I feel so alone, just managing the program and stuff. When something like that happens, I usually have my assistant coaches, who are male. But they're just like—I can go have a beer with them and shoot the shit. That's what it really is, but they don't get just what it means to be female, not necessarily for me, but what changes we need to make for these women.

Some coaches would never dream of having personal or social time with their male colleagues, as they found themselves up against much harsher male responses. Ella spoke about meetings where male colleagues would "just tune it out and [not] want to listen," but when I pushed her to give me more details on that and her additional comment that it makes her "not want to speak up," she went quiet, and said, "I'll have to think about it for a few." It is clear that such examples are painful for some women even to talk about.

Others, like Sarah, a D3 coach, recounted earlier days as a young assistant coach:

> He basically treated me like I was a water girl. I basically would just give water to the players when he needed. He never asked for my advice, he never asked me to run a drill, he never asked me to do any of that in my first year of working with him. I basically just kind of sat back and watched. There was a time my second year when we were in his office and we were talking about the fact that we were losing a lot of games. And he said, "Why isn't this working?" And I said to him, "I think you're over-coaching. I think you're giving them so much information that they don't know how to do it." And he threw a clipboard at my head.

I was astounded and asked, "Did he hit you?" to which Sarah coolly replied, "No, I ducked and it missed me." It is her reaction after recounting this story that surprised me the most. I asked her why she didn't retaliate or cry or scream:

> I think because of playing in middle school actually, with a men's team, I realized that just sitting back and watching and just kind of working towards what I wanted to work towards made me successful in what I was doing. So I kind of saw that as, he's gonna react how he wants to react, but I have a choice of how I react to it. And that was my decision.

She kept her composure because it was the only way she felt she could be successful. My research shows that some women, just like the young 11-year-old girls (see chapter 2), are putting their heads down, dealing with tons of pressure, and at times sucking it up, instead of exploding. The real question becomes: How long can they take it? And what will the mechanisms be that allow them to release the safety valve? Clearly, playing with the boys made them strong and skilled and yet one wonders what the cost was to their true identity and self-worth.

Other women faced similar anger, like Margaret when she first started her head coaching position. Without an assistant, her then-AD offered to help her and that is when the trouble started:

> I gave him my practice plans for preseason, so it was two weeks long. I was like, "Here are the times I want to practice." It was a typical early morning run, get them awake, we go eat breakfast as a team. We have a nice, relatively easy footwork session, a little technical session, just to get their feet going. And then we just play. I just want to evaluate them. And that was the first three days. I was perfect, it was four pages, double-spaced, it was great. And he started crossing off practices. He kept [nixing] practices: "You should change this time to this. No, no, no, start introducing this at this time." And then this is me going into this meeting, having already talked to our men's soccer coach, who I really trusted, and his practice plans were very similar to mine, so I thought, "Okay, I'm comfortable with this." And when I mentioned, "Ted, the men's soccer coach, is following this practice plan, why can't my girls?" "Oh it's too much for them, it's

too much for them." "Well, I went through this for my four years. We did triple sessions, my coach knew when to cancel sessions. I believe that I would know when my girls are hurting too much to practice and for us to do a recovery session; why can't we do that?" And he's like, "No, no, no, we're changing this. This cannot happen." And I said, "Are you saying this as my assistant coach, or as my AD?" And he jumped across the table—

During this interview, my mind was reeling about this newly hired, young female coach being alone with a male supervisor who seemed to be getting angry. I started to worry about what she was going to tell me. At this point, I actually interrupted her, to ask whether they were in her office space or his. Looking back at the transcribed data, I'm not sure why it would matter to me if they were in his or her office, I just knew I felt terribly worried about the outcome as she continues to recount her story to me:

No, we were in his office. It was kind of like a little coffee table, and he put both of his hands on the coffee table, and he goes, "I'm your AD. I tell you what to do." And I grabbed my practice plan and walked out. And I just—I didn't want to deal with it. I knew that if I opened my mouth, something bad would happen. And I wasn't even to my first practice yet. And so I walked out. Then I locked my door in my office, gave myself time to calm down. And then he came in. And he goes, "I want your practice plans for every single practice. You can keep the times and the numbers of practices you want per day, but I want your entire practice plan. Say we practice at 8? I want to know what you're doing at 8:01." And I was like, "That's totally fine. I'd do that anyway. I'll hand it to you." And I asked him again, "Are you asking for this as my assistant, or as my athletic director?" And he goes, "Athletic director. I need to know what my coaches are doing." And I'm like, "Are you doing this for other coaches as well or are you just doing this for me, because I'm new?" "Well, you're young. I just hired you." And then walked out.

FEMALE ALLIES

In some cases, building an ally network was much easier with female colleagues (although this was not always the case). Sarah remembers working under a woman who basically treated her as an equal:

> We had a great relationship. I think she saw the value of being with the program as long as I had and she didn't think that I was trying to take over the program, or that I saw myself as the head coach. I kind of let her set the tone of what she wanted to do and I just kind of followed with filling in how she wanted it. By the time of our second year, it was more like we were two co-coaches of the team.

Similarly, Ella remembered help from a female colleague. Upon arriving at one head coaching job (at the young age of 25), she found little help and had to try to ascertain how to get by:

> So I get there, I start meeting people, trying to figure out the lay of the land, trying to learn what the school's

about while also trying to send some emails out to the players and figuring out what I was going to do with my assistant coach. Trying to figure out what paperwork was around in terms of recruits and stuff like that. Because when I got there, all I had was a computer. There was nothing, I didn't even have a roster. I had to get a roster from the office manager because there wasn't even a roster on the desk or anything. I remember being like "Whoa!" because I feel if I were to leave a position, everyone wants to leave at least a roster, and some other info. It was pretty much just a computer and trying to dig that stuff up was the first week or so, trying to get that stuff done. Everyone was pretty helpful; the office manager, who is still there, is awesome. She took me everywhere I needed to go to get the paperwork signed, to figure out my computer. She was pretty key in terms of just being able to get sorted and settled. She was great.

Others, like Clara also found female colleagues helpful. She described her female AD when she first became a head coach:

I actually got along with her very well. She's one of these people that, if you ask 100 people about her, you're gonna get 50/50 as far as, some people love her, some people hate her. And that was the reality of it. As I said, she'd been here 42 years, she had a lot of her own policies, she was set in her way as to how she ran her department. And some people agreed with it and some people didn't. She's very, very well respected, she's one of the top Division 2 ADs in the country. They call her kind of the godmother of Division 2. And I got on very well with her. Like I said, I do think I'm one of these people that has a pretty good relationship with people. Some people were scared of her, some people were intimidated by her. The thing you had to know with her is, if you ever needed anything or asked for anything, you better know why you're asking and be prepared. Don't just walk in there and say, "Oh, I need this because of this." You better have it written out, know why you need it. I think she respected people that were good at their job too, and I'd like to consider myself good at my job. I knew how to handle the relationship with her, which allowed us to get on great for seven years.

Other women, such as Barbara, had also relied upon earlier female mentors who had influenced their career arc (see specific details about her mentor in chapter 5).

Yet female colleagues weren't always helpful. Sarah noted that after the flying clipboard incident, she didn't even tell her female AD:

I didn't feel comfortable with her, I didn't feel like she was a very supportive AD for anyone. And even as a student, I didn't feel like she was very supportive, so I never felt comfortable. I felt more comfortable with other coaches that I would talk to.

It's important to note here that many women returned to coach at the schools they played at during their undergraduate years. I think this pattern speaks to the tight-knit community and small boundaries of the soccer world in the U.S., as well as the routes that women often find. Women use their social capital, and how it is linked to their past successes. Many of them were encouraged to "come home" to their former institutions as they knew the campus environment, understood the overall athletic vision, and believed in the respective program. It appears that coaches want women to go back to what they know, and players want to go back to what they knew. Such returns were not always easy, though, as Kathy found returning to her alma mater. She left after senior year feeling a bit uncomfortable that she hadn't played much and then returned as an assistant coach to work with that same coach. She questioned his earlier motives. He eventually decided to retire, leaving the head coaching job to her, but she still wonders about his motives. It took her years to come to the decision that she was good enough. Such findings leave us wondering how many men find themselves in similar pathways, or if they are encouraged more often to branch out to bring new blood into new programs. This is an area of study that must be investigated sociologically in the near future.

One interesting addition in my data on female allies was that some coaches I met were offered the Senior Women's Administrator job titles within their athletic departments to help build such connections. The SWA position was created to help other women in their athletic career paths when the details on how to do that were often quite vague. Several coaches that I met held these SWA positions on their respective campuses. As Sydney explained to me, "It's part of the administration in any athletic department. Oftentimes, it could be a coach, and it's a woman that's prominent in the department, although I don't know if it's articulately defined anywhere, but who can handle being the liaison for female sports, any sports, just in regards to fairness and making sure that—they're not even Title IX representatives. They are supposed to be the liaison for women's sports, whatever the case may be." Yet the coaches I met who were given the titles were unsure about what that status meant or required. Margaret was told she would be given the SWA title, with additional duties, yet nothing ever came of the job. She wasn't able to find out specifics about details or funding to be the SWA. As she put it, "they ignored me," and the title means "absolutely nothing." Others, like Barbara, faced similar uncertainties surrounding the job. She noted, "I'm a Senior Woman Administrator, for which I have done nothing. So you're second highest female in the department. But I think it's just a title, for Title IX, because I haven't done anything with it." Sarah faced a very similar battle. She was told she was being given the title and job, but when she prodded for information and details, her administrators told her "never mind, we're not offering you the position anymore."

After my interviews with coaches who did mention such examples of inequality within their athletic departments, I would sometimes conclude, "Oh, okay, so gender really makes a difference then." Surprisingly, they would often respond with, "No, I'm not necessarily saying that." There was an interesting paradox in that they spoke vividly about inequalities and differences, but didn't want it to come down to gender. The "g" word seemed to scare them. I think coaches are afraid to talk about gender differences in the workplace for several reasons: possible retaliation; difficulty in attaining jobs in such a tight, small, soccer community; and overall stereotypes of being seen as a combative female. Some women, though, were not afraid of labels and thus fought strongly for what they thought was fair.

Before turning to women who fought battles within their departments for fair gender treatment, I should note that simple respect and non-threatening relationships go a long way to success for these coaches. In Sarah's case, her head coach's husband took a job abroad and so the coach asked Sarah to be interim head until she returned in two years. She ended up doing very well that year, taking her team to the conference championship game. When I asked how the team responded to the shift, her answer was very telling about what young athletes are looking for:

> We had an amazing year. After seven years of me being an assistant coach and kind of sitting back and seeing what other coaches had done and maybe what I would have done differently, my team was very supportive of it. They really wanted me to be the head coach. I was more outgoing than the [previous] head coach, so they actually felt more comfortable with me, because we would have more conversations together and I would give them more details than she would give them. They were very supportive of having me, so I think in that way, I felt inspired and comfortable to move into position, and didn't feel like, "Oh, what did I get myself into?" So we had the best season that the women's program has ever had. They had never made it to the championship. We made it to the championship and we lost in the championship game.

Her confidence inspired their confidence. That seems critical in these stories. We must ask ourselves, how we can inspire self-worth and courage in coaches, so that it filters down to players? How does the sport bolster and support female coaches, and, in other cases, how does it crush their confidence and abilities? It appears that social networks and social capital are key.

FIGHTING: SPEAKING THEIR MINDS TO STAY OR LEAVE

A few women did speak up about the inequities they saw in their athletic environments. One woman, Sydney, didn't worry about being labeled as a complainer, as she knew that her views were appropriate and valid. She simply did not feel that gender inequality was fair in any measure. I document the troubles she had with her first undergraduate coach in the previous chapter (see chapter 5). Her coach was dismissive and insensitive to the players' needs. Sydney noted that it was ruining the dynamics on the team:

> It came to a point my junior year, where I thought, "I don't want to do this anymore." I was going to transfer to keep playing. So that was the difference. We had lost, in three years, 14 people not to graduation. Fourteen girls left the team, so we're talking people who transferred out, left school completely, or just stopped playing. And these were recruited, scholarship athletes who gave up scholarships because that's how poorly the team was run, that's how bad the chemistry was, and by my junior year, I just thought, "This isn't right. I'm not going to endure this any longer." And I remember one of the things that he would do, because he loved to manipulate and play mind games, and if you were naïve to it or scared of it, you played into it. All this manipulation from this really ridiculous, egotistical, self-obsessed individual. All about him feeling important. I wasn't learning anything, and the team was totally dying.

She decided she was going to leave, but decided first to tell the administration about his verbally abusive behavior:

> I remember it vividly. It's not right. It's not fair that this man can be so manipulative, so unprofessional, so degrading, and ruin the experience of this young women's team. Absolutely it was based on gender. There was no doubt in my mind even then, it wasn't right. He treated us like crap, and he thought he could and nothing made my blood boil more than that. I was already leaving, but it was not right. And I remember sitting there with the AD, the assistant AD, we had meetings afterward where I was saying, "You need to know, there is a severe problem." And when I started to give them just tons of info and examples, they were floored. And then they started to call people in and get the same stories without my being there. So, no doubt about it, when I think about gender and equality, I was like, "This isn't right and I'm not gonna stand for it." Because he treated women like crap and he treated us like—and we were 18, 19, 20, and 21. So we were young women. And here's this man, responsible for our well-being, our happiness, and our success, and he abused it, and he did it because we were women. And from then to this moment, you probably see, I still get fired up about it. Because it's not okay. He ruined the love of the game. And he was ruining mine, and that I would not tolerate. But my teammates, some of them just left because they couldn't tolerate it anymore, but they lost the love of the game. And that I would not take. And that is probably from how I grew up, because we loved the game.

She recounted to me that he later got fired, at which point she told herself:

> Oh my God, I can get a fresh start. And that's what I did. I stayed. And who they hired stayed for the next 14 years and turned the program around within the year.

Yet Sydney, unfortunately, would face continued discrimination again later in her career. She eventually got an assistant job at a D1 school:

> From day one, I probably should have known there were issues. I went in, I remember sitting at my desk, and they didn't tell me anything to do and I just sat there and I kept saying, "Hey, do you guys need me to do anything?" Nope! And they just went about their work and I just sat there. And I stared at nothing.

In addition, these men made Sydney feel uncomfortable:

> So we had a player—this is one of the book of instances I could get into—but they would talk about the players sometimes in a sexual manner in this regard. One of our players hurt her back and they said, "Oh, I know why her back hurts, it's because her boyfriend was in town." And all those kind of things. So now it became sexual, which I'd never really had before. And these guys did it a lot. They talked about breasts, they would stare at women.

But the problems only escalated from there:

And to say I was miserable was an understatement. When you're going to work every day, I truly was the unhappiest I've ever been in my entire life before or since. I tried so hard to do whatever it took, and all it did was get worse. So even stroking the ego, because here I was, I need this job, I'm here where I want to be. Finally Division I and this was the difference—I loved the team. So you become close with the girls and you're the female presence for them.

I asked her for more details about the head coach:

[He] had a temper problem. He would just scream and yell, would flip out and storm off the field, get in his car, storm away. One time we were at a semifinal of our conference. We win the game. He was screaming for 80 minutes of that 90-minute [game] at one particular player. She came off and she's told me about it because he was a little bit of a loose cannon. He's a crazy man. And I always told the girls, well, I don't blame him, that's on us and that's on you, and you need to play regardless of what anyone says. So I would just be trying to build him up and I wouldn't even badmouth him because I don't want to do that. Not what I'm gonna do, it's gotta be a unified front. That's just mentality, but of course these—I don't want to be mean—but these unintelligent men don't understand any of that. So she came to talk to me, he's standing right there, and he had told me, "I want to know more of what they're saying to you." So here she's telling me, he's standing there hearing us. So I'm like, "Hey, you got a second?" He ends up kicking a ball bag, taking one of the vans that carried a third of the team, and driving off, leaving the team stranded. So we had to put a third of the team illegally into two other vans. People hitting the ceiling. Illegally. God forbid someone got in an accident.

Eventually the coach started having meetings with the team and assistants, without telling Sydney, asking her to do team laundry and even asking her to take the thirty players out to dinner alone on an away trip, so he could watch a game elsewhere with his male colleagues. She was devastated and alone, cognizant that it was very similar to her undergraduate experience, except now, as she put it "it was my profession, and they held my future."

She eventually went in to talk with her Senior Women's Administrator (SWA):

So, I go in, and I said, to the SWA—I talk. And she's like, "Sydney this isn't good." And I'm like, "it's awful and I can't take it anymore. This is awful, you need to know. I am leaving, I am not going down the same [road again]. I am not going down without letting you know that this is atrocious, and these men should not be coaching women. You need to know it." So then, they have a senior exit interview. They always have this exit interview, but I think they ask questions that are more pointed to me, so they learn I'm not lying, but they don't tell me that. And then they start to say, "Well, Sydney, we want you to stay. What can we do to make you stay? The kids love you, ba-ba-ba." And I'm like, "Are you insane? I'm not staying. What do you think is gonna change? You have to change this, this isn't just going to go away," which they don't love to hear. So they keep me, and now they start to investigate.

Later, she hired a lawyer:

> And then all of a sudden, things got done quickly. And the lawyer who heard my case said, "Sydney, this is really serious. What you're telling me—and you can even have the kids to attest to these scenarios—this could be a sexual discrimination suit against the university." I'm like, "I agree, but I don't want that. I just want what's fair for these girls. It's not about me, I don't care, I want to move on and get another job." That's what I told him. I don't want them to destroy my reputation, because [the head coach] was going to do it, and he did anyway.

She eventually got a settlement.

Sarah was another coach who wasn't afraid to speak her mind. She graduated from a D3 school, and then was asked to stay on as an assistant coach. Her head coach was focused on what she called "male coaching":

> He was very intense, very focused. He had worked with women's programs before, but I felt like he was much more focused on the male style of coaching, where it was focusing on teaching them every skill possible, and not how to come together as a team, which I feel like working with women is an important part to portray for them.

When Sarah stayed on after graduation to be his assistant coach, he became verbally abusive, throwing a clipboard at her (see earlier discussion in this chapter). What is remarkable about her story though is that she eventually developed a better relationship with him, when she realized that she simply shouldn't talk about his coaching style:

> The third year, he was better about working with me. He would ask my advice on some stuff and I would give it to him, but it would be comments on players or whatever. It was never on his coaching style. So, it was just different in how I approached working with him. And we had a fine working relationship in the third year. I think it was the best out of all three of them. And at the end, it was the last game of the season, he was going to resign. He said he was just waiting until the end of the game and then he was going to resign, so he had kind of told me all that, how it was going to play out.

She went on to recount how later in her career arc, she struggled to respect her male soccer counterpart coach as he seemed to hold so many offensive views about (see earlier sexist comments in this chapter under the Looking for Allies section):

> It's been very difficult working in that situation, because for one, it's totally against who I am and what I believe in and what we're trying to teach these students. So it's against that, but also it's kind of against me and I see how he feels about me and my role, and that he thinks we're just women and so he kind of thinks our program is a joke.

The administration later put her in an office with another male colleague which only led to more stress:

So they put us into an office together and he would moan at me and I'd say, "Hey, how's it going?" and he would just ignore me. Or I would be in the office and ask him a question, and he wouldn't answer it, or those type of behaviors that would go on. Like I would say, "How's everything going?" He'd say "muh." And that would be his answer to me. Or, "How's your recruiting going?" And he would turn around and walk out of the office. Or just ignore me. So that was for a year that we were in the office together.

Later the ADs offered her the SWA position, but when she asked for clarification on the job, they retracted the offer (see earlier in this chapter). The final straw came when they asked her, with only two weeks until the start of the season, to move out of the shared office into a space she calls a "closet office":

And that's when they said they were gonna take away my office and ask me to move. It used to be a closet, and they were gonna ask me to move into a closet.

I'm not on contract, and they asked me to move into this office, so then I wouldn't have access, because no one would be on campus until the end of August, so I wouldn't have my computer or my phone or any of that, because it wouldn't have been hooked up in time for me to get that. So I would have been working through preseason without all those things. So it was those type of things that they kept doing to me during that time.

They also took away my health insurance package. They had given me a health insurance package, but they were letting the men's coach stay on campus. They gave him housing and all his utilities and a meal plan with the part-time package, but they decided to take away my health insurance package

She later went to the administration and told them she was resigning, but they offered her mediation, not with an outside provider, but with five in-house male administrators and herself. She decided that was not real mediation and that she wanted to leave. Ironically, one person made her stay:

I went to check my email for the last time and I had an email from my athletic trainer that was just the nicest thing I have ever read, and just basically said, "You just need to know that we're here, as a family, and we're still your family." And at that point, I was like, "Why am I doing this, why am I leaving something so good for two people that mean nothing to me?" So I decided in that moment to stay. And I hadn't even talked to my husband about it. So he thinks I'm resigning and I walk into this meeting with this new understanding that I'm gonna stay, and I'm like, "I want an office outside of Athletics, I want a contract with you guys that says if I still am unhappy in November, that you guys will pay me 100% of my salary at that point, because I've done pretty much 100% of my work at that point." They pay over a pay scale and I knew at that point, I was gonna have done everything. So I had all of these, "This is what I want from you guys if I decide to stay." And they said yes to all of it. They said, "We'll put it in writing and have you come back in and sign it, and you'll stay through the season."

Another woman, Melanie, the D3 coach mentioned earlier, also ended up fighting a battle she didn't expect. Early on in her now ten-year job at the D3 school, she had a male AD that she states "was really good to me, so even in those first few years when I did get parent feedback that wasn't positive, that was really mean, he always had my back, because he really believed in what we were doing and where we were going." She went on to add:

> I thought about this a lot, and what I felt he did was, he valued the things about me that I value. And he was very into the way I did it, and because there were results, he was very good with it. He really valued how I led. Little examples: Like I had a kid that was not a good apple, and I ran her out of our program. And she's a goalkeeper. So I know losing her means I only have one goalkeeper on the roster the next year, but I so do not want her in my program. So coming into the next year, my one lone goalkeeper calls me over the summer to tell me she's been diagnosed with cancer. And she's good, like the end of the story is great. It was actually one of the more wonderful experiences of my life, but I'm like, "Oh shit!" I don't know how this is gonna turn out with this kid I love, and at the time, my mother had breast cancer too. "Shit! I don't have a goalkeeper." And the kid's like, "I'm coming back to school, I'm playing through this." But obviously, she could not play as much as she wanted. This kid is incredible. She would do a chemo treatment on Thursday, on Friday she would miss whatever we had because she's sick as a dog, and on Saturday, she's back with the team. She's

amazing, she's an incredible, incredible young woman. So that was amazing, but my boss, I never even thought about asking that other kid to come back to the team, the one that I'd run off. And he said to me, "I'm just so happy with the way you've handled this, because you didn't ask that kid to come back." And I had never even thought about that. So I just really felt seen by him.

Later, a new female AD was hired and Melanie was really excited to be "led by a woman," but found "it's the lowest level of leadership I've experienced as a professional." She went on to recount how their personalities were different, visions for resources were disjointed leading to two new assistant positions being created and given to different sports, not soccer. She started job searching, got a job offer, told the new female AD who told her, "You're lying," as she believed no one got a job offer on the spot. Melanie found this questioning of her integrity, along with the knowledge that her male soccer coach counterpart, who ironically also had just gotten got a job offer, parlayed his offer into a huge salary bump at his current institution as unacceptable. She ended up contacting a Title IX lawyer in California.

During the whole process, she reached out to a retired male friend, who had been the VP for student affairs when she was hired. They saw each other every so often for breakfast, and he told her, "You have to fight this," while simultaneously and ironically, a female colleague at a national coaching academy told her to "be really careful about this." Melanie felt that the woman was subtly advising her not to fight it. But Melanie plodded on and, after dozens of meetings and a formal gender equity assessment, they agreed to her pay raise. She told me:

It was International Women's Day, that's the day when it got resolved. It took three days for [the male coach] to get a $10,000 raise; it took me six months, but that's the process. It finally gets resolved, I get a new contract, and again, I've decided to be as kind as I can, so I honestly feel like my relationship with my boss is not necessarily authentic, but it's kind.

RETREATING

In rare cases, coaches talk about feeling so stressed that they thought about quitting or wondered how long they would actually stay in their positions. By the time I had finished writing this book, two coaches (out of 16) had officially quit and moved on to new jobs (both outside of collegiate coaching). In addition, one coach respondent I had been referred to had just resigned, and thus would not consent to be interviewed about her situation. I found though that it wasn't just the stories of the women who actually left that were most important, it was in fact those narratives from women who had thought about what leaving would mean that were most troubling. Several women spoke about walking away if they ever felt it was too much.

In my discussion with Hannah, she noted that she had thought about leaving, but wasn't always sure what she would do next. Yet she argues it is more than that:

> Well, you don't want to—they always say a coach should leave when they're on top, you know. I would not be satisfied with myself if I left now. I've thought about it, trust me.

Yet, when I asked her what she would possibly do, her answers seemed well thought out. She revealed that, in fact, she wants to stay to keep making a difference:

> There's a fear of what are you going to do next? I've devoted a lot of time to my career. I don't feel like that fear is holding me to this job; it's more about dissatisfaction with myself and how it's gone the last couple of years. And I've kind of, in my mind, given myself one or two more years to see if I can make some changes. And if it's the same as far as what I'm getting out of coaching, then I think it's a sign to move on. But if I start getting—I definitely have lost my love of what I was doing, and just dragging to work and stuff. And just in the last couple of weeks, with having just the underclassmen now, I've kind of rekindled that love. So I kind of want to see what comes of it. But definitely I have been thinking about career changes in the next few years. For me personally, I invest so much into this—like even my sense of self—and it's exhausting. I love it, but some days, it's just—I evaluate how my session goes. I take it so personally, so if a session goes well, I'm feeling great about myself. If it goes bad, my confidence goes down and I feel shitty. So it's that roller coaster and learning how to deal with that roller coaster.

Other coaches like Sarah want to resign and actually set the process in motion. They call HR, tell them they are done, but then in her case, she stayed (see previous section). Sarah was so unhappy and felt such little support from the AD at her school. He had taken away her office and her health insurance package, and she felt she had no recourse but to leave. Unfortunately, when she did tell the AD she was leaving, he made her feel guilty, telling her "This is one of the best jobs you could ever have in the whole wide world, please don't resign. I think you're gonna regret this."

Some, like Barbara, struggled without females to rely upon in her various jobs. In our interview she talked about loving her job, but wondered if she might eventually look for something else. She recounted three specific female colleagues that were difficult to work with:

> Those three females were my worst experiences. I never even thought about that... One was kind of self-explanatory. But the second one actually told me that she was intimidated by me. And I will tell you, myself and the other graduate assistant that was working with the team played at much higher levels than she did. And we were pretty strong voices in terms of what we thought should happen at practice. So when we would give feedback in meetings and things like that, she wouldn't have it, really. She wouldn't take our feedback and wouldn't listen. And we did crazy drills, and you could tell the players didn't even really enjoy what they were doing. And she didn't last very long there... There was just a lack of communication and things like that. And it was a struggling season in terms of feeling like our input was valued. And then, the third female that I worked with, basically again, it was just an appreciation factor.

These coaches struggle with little to no agency, with less power needed to do the job, and less credibility than expected.

The majority of these coaches have few mentors in their new environments, little knowledge of how the "old boy's network" operates, meaningless titles (such as the SWA positions), and little overall support. Given the volatile and unique territories they find themselves in, they use multiple strategies to change the outcome of the battle: they look to others who have mentored them; they fight back verbally against the sexism; and in some cases they retreat partially or completely.

What is unique from my findings is that in this chilly climate the coaches "do gender" in unique ways. They do not typically engage in the Queen Bee syndrome, even if other women do so (as Barbara's aforementioned quote reveals). I believe that such findings are critical for women outside of the athletic realm. Much more research needs to be done on how and why these women create such nurturing environments for other female soccer players coming up through the ranks. We need to document what those specific frameworks are and how they could in turn shape the lives of other women around the globe outside of sports.

In addition, this chapter reveals that male and female collaborative efforts are valuable, and actually critical in the workplace. These coaches do not turn primarily to female support—as there are few females there—thus their actions and behaviors speak loudly about our male colleagues. How and why do men choose to be gender aware, and what do such relationships look like? Further research needs to be done on these gender-aware men (similar to what Arlie Hochschild [1989] called "modern men" in her historical analysis of housework) and how we might develop greater awareness amongst all men in the soccer and non-soccer worlds. Such research will also allow us to focus on the hugely positive attributes that might blossom when men and women do gender research together. Such research has often raised feminist questions about whether women really need men to accomplish said projects, and if having men along for the ride is a detriment to women's independence, ability, and equality? I actually turn such questions on their heads and ask the opposite: Why shouldn't we ask men along for the ride? There is actually much that they can learn from us in all fields and walks of life! (The problem might be getting them to want to join the gender fight.) The example of GO BEECHWOOD (see chapter 2) showed that indeed some men care strongly about women's issues and lives and *are* willing to help further our goals. In addition, the GB project showed that having a male counterpart brought a vital, external perception of validity to the project. I saw this as clearly evident when my male colleague moved out of state and I struggled to have my solitary voice heard within the Beechwood soccer club regarding the GB work. Seemingly, his presence and acceptance of the project said to other males that the project was good, valuable, and cogent. After he left, the validity of this gender work seemed to be questioned, and it felt more like a battle for recognition and acceptance. I would like to argue that as a woman I didn't need that male influence and voice, but in this male domain of soccer, I found that I did. My work raises positive possibilities of male-female collaboration. If in fact, women get farther with male input and their stamp of approval (due to entrenched, outdated views in the workplace), working together with men can enable women to open up new doors to innovative projects and cutting-edge research. Such positive potentials could be really valuable to female-forward projects across the globe. The real question becomes, how do we bring more gender-aware men to the table? And even more importantly than that, how do we get more men to care about women in sports, and gender issues in the first place? How do we get men to further women's causes, without making the gender issues seem like an added on agenda item, as opposed to an integral, coherent gender vision within youth clubs and soccer teams?

Chapter 7

Conclusions: Looking Ahead
Another Forty Years

THE AMERICAN WOMEN WON
THE WORD CUP THE FIRST
FEW TIMES IT WAS PARVED.
THEN THE OLMPIC GOLD,

So where will girls be in the next ten or twenty years in terms of youth soccer? Author Joe Drape (2018) pointed out in a *New York Times* article that in 2018 young kids' soccer participation (ages 6-12) is dropping significantly in the U.S. Such numbers must be looked at carefully, as they are younger than the ages of my respondents, but his commentary is still critical in this gender discussion. Drape points out the high cost of travel soccer, but gives few clues as to whether or not the number of girls participating is dropping more quickly than the number of boys. It seems that over the years I was collecting this data, our soccer numbers were shifting, particularly for little kids. So, if young kids aren't participating as much, that could have interesting ramifications for girls. On the one hand, we know that girls start sports later and often drop out earlier (Sabo & Valiz, 2008), so one wonders if their numbers will continue to grow as we look ahead to the future, or if they will drop, aligning with Drape's evidence of young player attrition. If the younger kids' attrition is primarily boys that are dropping out, could we see a huge shift—and advantage—for girls? Either way, the shifting sands seem to imply huge gender implications within sport, particularly youth soccer.

As we think about the expectations and experiences of the next crop of young athletes, it is important to think about the 96 women I met in this book. The middle school girls I met as young, slightly awkward 11-, 12-, and 13-year-olds back in 2014 are now in high school. Some of those girls made their varsity teams their freshman year of high school, while others played on the JV teams. There are probably some that did not choose to play in high school. Additionally, some of the high school girls I met several years ago, just finished their freshman or sophomore years in college. It would be interesting, if I had the time, to follow up with all of these engaging young women in five years to see how their views on being a f/athlete have changed or stayed the same.

Then there are the collegiate coaches. As mentioned in chapter 6, as far as I know, most of them are still at their same jobs; while two coaches have moved on to new jobs outside the head coaching realm. Studying the continuing arc of their professions would also be valuable as it would allow for a wider investigation of identity, profession, and gender. Certainly much has transpired in the last four years for all of these women, and their lives will continue to change and transform as they acquire new degrees or new positions.

My goal in this last chapter, however, is not to analyze where those career arcs might end up, but rather to look back at my findings and delineate a variety of solutions for the problems that I revealed through their stories and narratives.

My work has shown that the town greens, recreation parks, and school athletic fields are sites of dynamic (yet often hidden and unrecognized) gender work. The gender work that is being done there by young girls and women is not only vibrant and exciting, but is also a silent struggle that in many ways is bearing incredibly positive future changes for many more women. What this research brings to light is the important and dynamic personal and cultural growth for each of these females from youth to middle age. The players and coaches that are seemingly blossoming in the United States today are, on the one hand, a positive sign, but these data don't unearth the true stories and experiences behind the expanding rosters. Now that my research names these gender issues, I hope we can start more invested and intensive conversations about females in sport (particularly in soccer) that do not revolve around USWNT players, discussions over pay-to-play models in club soccer, professional female leagues abroad, or quantitative survey analysis data. My hope is that this qualitative research opens up not only a broader conversation about gender identity and sport, but a wider discussion about how we fare in career environments that aren't always inviting or easy to exist within as solitary females.

My book is not a how-to manual for surviving in a male world, but rather exposes the inequities that exist within one part of that world. This research illuminates the multi-layered pressures of girls in youth sports, the problem of over-invested parents, collegiate athletes who feel like second-class citizens, and female coaches who strive to make a difference yet often exist in athletic departments with few female allies.

It is important to note that this soccer world is not all negative. The women I met—no matter their age—loved many things about being there and felt that the struggles were worth it. The story of women in soccer then is not a story that is sheer doom and gloom, in fact—just the opposite—it is one of grit, perseverance, and hope. Yet I would be remiss if I didn't look back and try to offer up solutions to the dilemmas faced by young girls and women within the male domain of soccer today.

So what will the expectations and experiences look like for the next crop of young athletes and coaches? As I look ahead to solutions to the issues raised here, I believe we must focus on qualitative data to better understand the experiences of players and coaches within American soccer today. If we are to retain these newest, youngest players within this beautiful game, we must do a better job at analyzing gender in youth sports. Such data cannot only come from large broad-based survey data, but must be generated from in-depth qualitative analysis. Only then can we hear the stories behind the figures. Such data collection could be done locally (and cheaply) by pairing local soccer clubs with social science students at local colleges and universities and relying upon research methods classes at local universities who might need a semester-long project that focuses on local or national issues. Such applied sociology work would not only generate lots of data on gender issues in local sports clubs (even beyond soccer), but would also build stronger connections between sociology students and their wider community. Such bridge-building activities would be akin to service-learning projects in which both parties benefit from the ongoing research.

Second, we must address how and why girls are feeling pressure to be the "uber" girl in middle and high school. Such hidden pressures are terrifying given the recent surge in suicides in the U.S. (see Tavernise article). We must address girls' hidden stressors at the personal, academic, and sport levels. For this monumental task, I think that clubs focused on youth sport must look to broader models of addressing young women's needs. Here I return to the GO BEECHWOOD model for inspiration. Although clearly GB will not help every teenage girl and her multitude of pressures, it can be a place for young women to feel supported, learn to recognize their voices, and find a supportive community to encourage those voices. Programs like GB can be instrumental in supporting girls' inner lives that often get ignored in youth sport spaces. If we only conceptualize girls as petty, loud, indignant, and troublesome, we will miss out on a wealth of information about them as full, complete human beings. Whether we like it or not, girls do not step onto the field in the same way as boys (see general literature in Appendix I on girls in soccer). Thus, we must reach out to girls in unique ways that support their needs and concerns. Such programs cannot be a simple add-on service, whereby sports clubs say that they cater to girls but only offer events a few times per year. Rather, programs such as those like GB need to be an integral part of a club environment that is generated from the ground up. All clubs are not like Beechwood Soccer, and therefore the players at your respective club may have unique, specific needs or desires based upon your region, location, club structure, or coaching staff. It is vital that club administrators listen to these girls' voices to move club gender progress along. Club administrators may feel nervous or uncertain about how to address their gender concerns and build a program to support girls' needs. Here again, it is especially important that clubs reach out to their local community colleges and universities to rely upon the social science community for research advice, and help with data collection. Young, budding students in social science classes would be more than happy to build those links and bridge-building research connections. The result of such ties will be incredibly fruitful for both parties.

In addition, another critical piece for programs such as GB would be to open up a discussion with young girls about #MeToo, the social and political movement created in the wake of Harvey Weinstein's sexual harassment scandal. They are seeing the headlines on social media, but do teenage girls really understand the complexity of these gender issues? I would argue that most likely do not. In fact, it turns out that even most adult women don't always know what to do regarding sexual harassment; in fact, their most common response is to not report it. Feldblum and Lipnic, co-chairs of the Select Task Force on the Study of Harassment in the Workplace (2016) note in their report that

> in fact, based on the empirical data, the extent of non-reporting is striking. As with all the evidence we discuss in this report, almost all of the data on responses to harassment come from studies of sex-based harassment. Common workplace-based responses by those who experience sex-based harassment are to avoid the harasser (33% to 75%); deny or downplay the gravity of the situation (54% to 73%); or attempt to ignore, forget, or endure the behavior (44% to 70%). (pps.20-21)

So, if adult women aren't reporting negative treatment, it is highly unlikely that young teenage girls would do so for themselves. We must remedy this problem. GB, and programs like it, **should not** be political platforms, per se, but rather safe spaces where national and local experts can talk with girls about issues such as sexual inequality and discrimination. We hope that girls will speak up at the first sign of inequality, but it appears that many teenage girls may not know if action needs to be taken, or may simply feel unsure of the exact next steps to take.

Models like GB may, in fact, be the place where we not only enable girls to find their voices off the field, but also a place where we can have in-depth conversations about gender inequity and sexism. Such spaces are critical for young girls in this volatile gender climate. If clubs encourage girls to discuss gender and inequity in sport, it might be a way for young women to address how difficult the structural barriers are that they will face as older collegiate women and later as full-time working women.

Next, we must address the problems of over-invested parents in youth sport. This problem is so large it is almost impossible to begin to tackle, but tackle it we must. I posit that, instead of simply telling sports parents to "*shut* up," we must actually get them to *speak* up—in the correct setting. I think we should encourage more sports parents to actually get involved in club board work, so that they truly see what happens off the field in various facets of youth sport. Boards tend to be male-driven and male-dominated, and yet I argue that if we had more women (and gender-aware men) flooding boards with their skills, we might find more solutions for young f/athletes[31]. Parents often do not know the full extent of what happens off the field or at the soccer club boardroom table. Having more parents sign up for Board of Directors duties might enrich their broader vision of youth sport.

---

31 I do not, however, believe that we should just flood club boards with women simply because of their gender. Club soccer boards need women, and men, who *genuinely* care about, and can advocate for, girl's causes.

In her 2015 article, "Youth Sports Organizations: Six ways to increase accountability, transparency," Brooke DeLench argues that aside from running for a board seat, parents should push for a parent advocacy group (PAG) that "provides the board with feedback (both negative and positive) from other parents" (p. 1).

Yet, there is another piece of this puzzle, which is the Board of Directors' vision. Boards tend to be male-dominated, and need to develop a true, genuine gender vision. A picture at the top of Jena McGregor's *Washington Post* article (April 24, 2018) shows Katherine Graham in 1975 at a board meeting of the Associated Press Board of Directors. The picture shows Graham, the solitary woman dressed in a bright aqua blue dress with brown heels, surrounded by no less than 22 males in grey business suits. McGregor writes that "more than 40 years later, many boards in America still look much like this" (p. 1). I would argue that although youth sports board meetings are far from the Associated Press meetings in the wood paneled boardrooms of the 1970s, they still show a predominance of males with a smattering of females interspersed at the table. I often wonder just how many female presidents of youth soccer clubs there are in the U.S. This is yet another piece of future research that needs to be examined, along with how the women that are there presently fare within the boards of youth sport. Are they there as tokens? Do they end up taking on more job responsibilities than men? Are they often playing out traditional female roles such as secretary, fact checker, fundraiser, or golf tournament organizer? (Such findings would resonate with the work of Jo Welford (2011)). Moreover, are they talked over and their ideas dismissed, or do they actually have an active, genuine voice within meetings? Sheryl Sandberg (2013) encourages women in such positions to "lean in" at the table, but they can only make a difference if men listen to them when they do. We can lean in all we want, but if men at the table aren't willing to hear it, it means nothing.

I believe that there is another positive aspect to women entering these board positions. I posit that with more women entering boards, we might find more ways for greater cross-gender collaboration within clubs. Such collaborative efforts are not only a hugely positive step for creating change, but are a wonderful model for young girls (and boys) that change *can* happen with gender-aware men. It seems that in this #MeToo environment, young girls need to remember that plenty of men in America actually do want to help girls' causes and efforts. In addition, given the backlash women have faced within this cultural climate, such gender conversations will send a strong, positive message to young boys and males about what women really think, feel, and believe. Cross-gender collaboration could be incredibly fruitful in the sporting world. In an article on CNBC.com, Courtney Connley reported that new research shows that 41% of men haven't even heard of the #MeToo movement, and 47% haven't discussed it with anyone at all (Connley 2018). Such numbers seem shockingly high to me, and extremely troubling. Connley quotes one respondent in the study who said:

> Most men are unsure of how to handle speaking to women on a normal basis. Now they are even more unsettled and confused about how to approach a woman, handle a conversation, or give a compliment. Some have said that the movement may not have a true, lasting effect. (p.1)

Gender collaborations will, obviously, not solve all of the issues brought up in the #MeToo movement but they would be a good place to start building these positive, cross-gender, professional working relationships. Women and men working together on club board projects that focus on female development could be an easy way to initiate such conversations, and just as importantly, present good cross-gender role modeling for young athletes (both female and male). The beauty here is that both males and females would have much to learn from each other in this cross-gender work.

The real dilemma in these types of ventures is making sure that clubs are truly committed to gender change, as opposed to just offering lip-service advocacy. If we don't have youth sports clubs who really can stand behind their statements of helping young girls, we will only have add-on gender components that really don't meet young girls' fullest needs.

In addition, we need to determine how to change the social environments of f/athletes on college campuses. Such a solution will be neither easy nor quick. The one place that I believe we need to start is through educating our male collegiate students. The aforementioned flipped mentoring and collaborative project ideas are good places to start for young males to encounter gender issues that are real and pervasive. Yet people must think of ways to start a broader conversation about young men and misogyny. This conversation will need to occur in schools, athletic clubs, and family homes.

Finally, I argue that we must look to female coaches as a model for stamping out the Queen Bee syndrome in the world today. We must use their examples to view how and why they don't let female rivalry and competition stop their collaborative efforts. In turn, their experiences will help us further e-mentoring as a positive model for women in many other fields. My work exposes what strategies they use, but does not investigate their actions more deeply. Further research should look at what mentoring gives to the mentor and mentee in this situation and how such benefits might be translated into other professional fields. In addition, we need greater investigation into what it is in sport that enables these women to not feel compelled to engage in the Queen Bee syndrome.

One could argue that it is the competition within sports that allows women to feel less threatened, yet as there is plenty of competition in business such an analysis does not hold much weight. One might argue that it is the camaraderie of a team that brings a unique setting and culture to sports environments, yet here again the team dynamic in contemporary business fields might negate this idea as well. Clearly, a future study needs to be initiated on why collegiate coaches are so willing to pave the way for younger female athletes.

As I look back on the women and girls I've met over the last four years, I realize that their stories are so much more complex than the simple, progressive, and engaging image of females running in town parks, recreation fields, and collegiate athletic complexes. Their experiences are actually multilayered composites of complex gender behavior; both looking at and simultaneously avoiding gender. Seeing hundreds of young girls filling parks today as full-fledged athletes tackling defenders and putting goals into the back of soccer nets is an exciting statement about where girls are headed in youth sport in America today. Similarly, seeing and hearing women all over the country animated about being head varsity coaches at D1, D2, and D3 schools is a reflection of how women are breaking the grass divide on the soccer pitch.

It has been almost fifty years since Title IX was enacted in 1972 to enable girls (and boys) to play sports in discrimination-free environments. Information from the NCAA.org website shows that the law was put into effect so that:

1. "Women and men be provided equitable opportunities to participate in sports. Title IX does not require institutions to offer identical sports but an equal opportunity to play" (p.1).

2. "Female and male student-athletes receive athletics scholarship dollars proportional to their participation" (p.1).

3. "Other benefits: Title IX requires the equal treatment of female and male student-athletes in the provisions of: (a) equipment and supplies; (b) scheduling of games and practice times; (c) travel and daily allowance/per diem; (d) access to tutoring; (e) coaching, (f) locker rooms, practice, and competitive facilities; (g) medical and training facilities and services; (h) housing and dining facilities and services; (i) publicity and promotions; (j) support services; and (k) recruitment of student-athletes" (p.1).

Clearly, my work shows that gender inequality and differences still exist despite the law. So, what is next? Where will female youth sport—particularly soccer—be in the next 46 years in 2064? Will girls still believe that youth soccer clubs do not treat them equally to boys? Will there be more female collegiate head coaches? Will soccer clubs have figured out a way to engage in collaborative action to promote female players? Or will girls have decided to hang their cleats up due to the persistent gender inequality within said clubs and colleges? I dearly hope that is not the case, and I believe it won't be, if we listen to their stories and take them to heart. These young girls and women want to leave their mark on the field. They want to be remembered as being incredible athletes, committed teammates, and enduring role models for rising, younger female cohorts. So, I leave you with a call to action—get up out of your colorful folding chairs, get off the gender sidelines, and commit to making as much of a difference for women off the field as they are trying to make on it.

Appendix

An Annotated Bibliography on Literature Related to Female Athletics

GENERAL LITERATURE ON FEMALE PLAYERS IN SOCCER

Soccer and girls have not always been mentioned together. Sue Lopez's groundbreaking book *Woman On the Ball* (1997) is a key starting point for the historical analysis of women and soccer history. She outlines the last 100 years of women's unfair treatment at all echelons within the soccer hierarchy that kept them from being fully involved in the "world's magical sport." Her work documents how British women cracked open a door in a sport long equated solely with males. In the 21 years since the publication of Lopez's book, soccer research has certainly evolved, though it remains narrowly focused on how the male-dominant sport is changing due to women's presence as opposed to women's experiences in these aforementioned soccer teams and clubs.

Jo Welford's work (2011) sets the stage for examining the resistance that happens when those women in male-dominated clubs push for a broader, critical gender discourse. Her work shows us that women have often entered in non-playing roles, have had less media attention if they did get to play, are surrounded by predominantly male coaches and administrators, and are often underrepresented in decision-making within the hierarchy of the clubs.

Jayne Caudwell (2011) moves one step further than Welford by adding diversity and subjectivity into the analysis. Caudwell argues that gender is socially constructed, and explores how women are not a unitary group, as they don't "share the same location or gendered identity," since gender is both shared and non-shared (p. 334). Given this, women's specific, lived experiences become critical to her gender analysis. Caudwell uses the phrase "footballing femininities" to explore the complex layers of the female athlete, unearthing subjects as varied as the rigid boundaries between the sexes in terms of football governance and media coverage, and the frequent sexualization of female players. She also pushes us to see multiple feminisms instead of just one feminism, and implores us to look beyond the current definitions and frameworks of simply adding in feminism and femininity to national discourse to be more critical in our thinking and look to "difference, diversity, and deconstruction" (p.339). Her work then challenges us to study the situated, unique experiences of varied young women and girls in the sport.

In addition, Ruth Jeanes' work (2011) analyzes "alternate scripts of femininity" (p. 402), the interwoven fluid, dynamic constructions of gender identity as performance. Her concept of the "performing girl" speaks to the diversified meaning of being a girl in the 21st century, and this book strongly resonates with her findings.

There is a subset of literature that focuses on girls' distinct qualitative perspectives as female athletes, but it is limited. Alicia Milyak's work (2010) clearly points out that boys and girls don't experience sports in the same way, noting that "their abilities, tactics, and team dynamics are different" (p. 51). She argues that coaches must deal with males and females differently because of disparate physiological differences, resulting in radically different speeds, strengths, and injuries for each gender. In addition, her work points out distinct, valuable psychological differences, as girls value team chemistry and fitting in within teams so strongly. Neil Hull's work (2010), just a few months later, builds upon Milyak's research, and shows that, due to these team- and group-focus perspectives, girls tend to understand coaching instructions differently than their male counterparts. He argues that girls hear instructions in the context of the "greater good of the team" and are much more sensitive to the social dynamics (p. 28). Such findings encourage us to ask female players what they are thinking and feeling about their experiences, and to move beyond seeing club athletes as genderless players who are all the same.

The research of Fielding-Lloyd and Mean (2011) adds two important variables into the literature: confidence and responsibility. These authors note that women have certainly increased in numbers in English football clubs, yet have rarely been seen in leadership positions. They argue that "male-defined practices still dominate sport" (p. 346), and thus masculine clubs are still engaging in boundary keeping, by which men are still in control of club structures and cultural identity. As such, two narratives then become prevalent: female coaches are often seen as "less confident or able" (p. 350), and women are the ones responsible for change within the club (p. 357). The authors note that we must push beyond biological and historical notions of females as simply "different" within these clubs, to greater depths of research by asking, "How are they different?"

Other studies, such as those done by Atkins, Johnson, Force, and Petrie (2013), look beyond internal characteristics of girls and women as athletes to external influences. Atkins et al note that parents are a primary influence in determining happiness for female athletes, within what they call a "motivational climate" (p. 330). If parents are perceived as warm and supportive, girls' levels of enjoyment went up (p. 339). Similarly, girls' likelihood of staying in a sport increased if they were having fun, while boys stayed in the sport if they had "high perceptions of their ability and sports competence" (p. 340). Such findings remind us of the importance of intrinsic versus extrinsic motivational differences among male and female athletes.

A study done by Keathley, Himelein, and Srigley (2013) examines female and male player beliefs about the benefits and challenges of playing soccer, and more specifically why the rates of attrition for girls is much higher within sports. The authors found that time demands were a primary reason for both boys and girls to leave, but found that negative coaching experiences heavily influenced girls' decision to leave. Girls also more strongly emphasized the value of social relationships and connections through playing a sport, and psychological differences for men and women in sport point to what the authors call a "relational orientation" for girls as athletes (p. 171). The authors argue three strategies for improving the retention of girls: recruitment of coaches knowledgeable about gender issues, attentiveness to team dynamics, and reevaluation of pressure on high-level youth athletes.

What this brief glance at current literature shows is that there is value in studying youth soccer—as Paul Kooistra noted in his 2005 American Sociological Association paper—and that we need much more academic research on gender, soccer, and athletics. In addition, we need more qualitative, feminist analyses to explore how the female athlete is produced and subsequently how they are faring (see Caudwell 2011).

LITERATURE ON FEMALE ATHLETES

The literature on female players is divided into categories on health and injury prevention, fitness and performance determinants, and the gender-athlete paradox (the struggle to be both feminine and athletic). The largest segment of the most recent literature appears to focus on what shapes overall female player performance (Fanchini, Ghielmetti, Coutts, Schenna, & Impellizzeri, 2015); the role of mental toughness (Danielsen, Rodahl, Giske, & Heigaard, 2017), physiological performance (Mara, Thompson, Pumpa, & Ball, 2015), speed (Haugen, Tonnessen, Hisdal, & Seiler, 2014) and conditioning (Polman, Walsh, Bloomfield, & Nesti, 2004); and overall fitness determinants (Mujika, Impellizzeri, & Castagna, 2009).

In the category of health and injury prevention, there is analysis on how female coaches can prevent injuries among their players such as ACL tears (Vescovi & VanHeest, 2010); how psychological characteristics are risk factors in injuries for female players (Steffen, Pensgaard, & Bahr, 2009); and how kinetics shape female motion (Vescovi & Favero, 2014).

Finally, there is a growing body of literature on the gender-athlete paradox. Researchers are intrigued by the conflictual identity struggle for women to be simultaneously strong, muscular athletes and women that express femininity and its ideals. The earliest work on this conflict seems to appear post-1999, after the USWNT (United States Women's National Soccer Team) won the World Cup in California. Brandi Chastain's celebratory slide and the image of her removing her shirt, revealing her sports bra, unleashed a discourse about women's bodies as athletes. Schultz (2004) argues in her article on femininity and sports bras that such clothing items allow women to both exhibit the new ideal of toned, female athletic bodies while appealing to the ever-present "objectifying gaze" (p. 194). George (2005) moves a bit further, and talks about a performance body and an appearance body, noting that women display each one based upon various situations and contexts. Others such as Musto and McGann (2016) find that the majority of female collegiate athletes present themselves in feminine ways (long, styled hair draped in front of shoulders) in their NCAA roster photos despite being in athletic uniforms. They argue these women adhered "overwhelmingly to conventional feminine standards of beauty" (p. 105). Roth and Knapp (2017) add to this analysis of f/ athletes' public portrayals by exploring how they analyze and accept their athletic body types as women, and the role of their strength and conditioning coaches in that process. The authors argue that such coaches are critical individuals for teaching young women about confidence coupled with strength (p. 58). Kassing's (2017) work takes a different tact, focusing on the creation of SoccerGrlProbs, a YouTube series that uses humor to examine how female soccer players straddle the femininity and athletic divide.

LITERATURE ON FEMALE COACHES

While there is a growing amount of literature on female players around the globe, there is a dearth of literature on the lived, daily social experiences of female coaches. Much of the literature that does exist on female coaches is divided into categories focusing on barriers for female coaches, particularly in terms of inequality and sex discrimination; the role of gender stereotypes in attitudes and perceptions of athletes about coaches; and finally the role of homophobia in the experiences of female coaches. Not surprisingly, the largest body of material focuses on the various aspects of inequality and discrimination that female soccer coaches face.

In this large category of work, we see barriers that women face within the work environment. Acosta and Carpenter (1985) document the struggle female coaches have in regard to the "good old boys network"(1985) and thus find that there are few female role models to turn to in those environments (1988). Amelie Knoppers (1987) examines the structural context for female coaches, looking at the role of opportunity, power (and women's lack thereof in both categories), and gender proportion within the workplace. She notes that women face sex discrimination, lack the ability to mobilize resources, and at times may suffer from aloneness. Knoppers argues that there are "psychic costs of being a woman in a profession with a skewed ratio (male to female)" (p. 18). Acosta and Carpenter argue more recently (2009) that we've made progress, but that many roadblocks still exist: "compensation, time, respect, and will" (p. 23).

In a 1991 study, Donna Pastore noted that female coaches have a hard time balancing work, life, and family with a high-stress job. Similarly, Inglis, Danylchuk, and Pastore (1996) note that work balance and conditions, recognition and collegial support, and inclusivity affect why intercollegiate college coaches stay or leave. Cooper, Hunt, and O'Bryant (2007) concur that women find fewer role models and networks, but additionally show that women face lower salaries and a struggle to balance family life with work.

Sadly, little progress seems to have been made over the last three decades, as Donna Lopiano (Women Sports Foundation report, 2016) finds that women have "fewer professional advantages than their male counterparts, earn lower salaries than their male counterparts, have less of a voice, and face more tenuous job security" (2016, p. 5).

One fascinating finding in this literature is the presence of the paradox of the contented working woman. Cunningham and Sagas (2003) show through quantitative analysis that despite distinct work discrimination (lower pay, thwarted career advancement opportunities), women still express positive work attitudes. The authors refer to the work of Parks, Russell, Wood, Robertson, and Shewokis (1995) who posited that maybe women in male-dominated professions feel they are pioneers (Cunningham & Sagas, p. 463). Later findings by Derks in 2011 show similar patterns with women in high-level positions at male companies often downplaying "the pervasiveness of gender discrimination" (p. 1247). Such findings raise the question of whether qualitative analysis would reveal more nuanced thoughts on these matters and why women tend to not want to call out discrimination.

Similarly, Leanne Norman's (2013) work shows that female coaches feel they have "strenuous demands" (p. 11) and get "little reward in return for a heavy workload" (p. 12). Her work raises the question of where women in such environments turn for social networking support.

Allen and Shaw's work (2013) adds to the examination of specific working environments for female coaches. They point out that research tends to focus on difficulties and career developments, but rarely on exact working environments. Using self-determination theory, they examine four themes in female coaches' narratives: relationships with personnel; learning and development opportunities; relationships among coaches; and the coach as a person (p. 1). My work most closely relates to this piece of critical literature, but it is not clear what type of sport organization they are studying.

Kilty's work (2006) on barriers and challenges shows that female coaches experience internal barriers of perfectionism; lack of assertiveness; and difficulty in creating a balance between life, work, and family (p. 226); and external barriers such as a lack of mentors, being seen as incompetent, and homophobia (pps. 224-225). Her findings show that female coaches need greater mentoring and support, coupled with more professional development opportunities.

A final barrier that comes up in this section of the literature is that of homologous reproduction, a term first delineated by Rosabeth Moss Kanter in 1977 and applied to sport by many including Cunningham, Sagas, and Teed in 2006. Homologous reproduction is the notion that the dominant group will "strive to guard their power and privilege" (Kanter, p. 48) by reproducing themselves within the organization. Kanter argued historically that "there is a development of exclusive management circles closed to 'outsiders,' [as]... bureaucracies are social inventions that supposedly reduce the uncertain to the predictable and routine" (p. 48). Such social frameworks are found in many institutions, including global and national sport in 2019, whereby anyone who does not reproduce those gendered identities and roles is seen as a problem and a disadvantage to the organization. Unfortunately, women are seen as dismantling the normative gender framework in sport (see similar findings in Caudwell 2003, pp. 376-377). In addition, homologous reproduction echoes the findings in the literature on Queen Bee syndrome (see analysis in chapter 6). Kanter's historical work was written before a time when women were breaking numerous corporate glass ceilings and entering into the upper echelon of business. Queen Bee syndrome looks at how women are now guarding the inner circles of management by keeping younger women out of the top of the corporate hierarchy.

Secondly we find literature that focuses on how gender stereotypes shape views and experiences of coaches. Fasting and Pfister (2000) note that female players are more satisfied with female coaches as they see them as more communicative and better attuned psychologically, and that "many people take for granted that a top-level coach is a man" (p. 92). Fielding-Lloyd and Mean (2011) explain essentialist views for why there are so few female coaches by exploring two gendered discourses: women as less confident and women as responsible for change within clubs. Schlesinger and Schlesinger's (2012) work in Germany rounds out the work on female barriers, revealing the mechanisms of gender stereotypes (e.g., men have instrumental qualities and women have expressive qualities) that help to keep women out of these coaching education positions. The authors argue that women's legitimacy is often questioned, thus creating an organizational culture where men have to prove their incompetency before losing acceptance, but where women need to demonstrate their competency first (p.61). Madsen, Burton, and Clark's work (2017) shows that much like the work of Schlesinger, athletes viewed masculine traits as more valuable for a head coach position (p.136) and male athletes in particular "rated feminine characteristics as less important for coaches" (p. 137). Such findings point to social attitude barriers that exist even before women get offered jobs as head coaches. These entrenched views are embedded in athletic departments and sports environs long before they show up.

One glaring omission that we find in literature in the U.S. is a focus on work contexts, situated narratives, and research on D2 and D3 coaches. There is research on D1 coaches (see Kamphoff, Armentrout & Driska, 2010; Welch & Sigelman 2007), yet few studies focus on qualitative analysis, instead depending upon surveys and questionnaires, and very few studies include any analyses of D2 and D3 coaches.

The last category of work on female coaches relates to homophobia within female sports (see Greendorfer & Rubinson 1997, Griffin 1992, Caudwell 1999, Norman 2012, and Keats 2016). Greendorfer and Rubinson (1997) present a pivotal overview that documents general information on homophobia, along with more detailed studies on physical educators and homophobia, homophobia and the media, and the connections between lesbianism and sport, and heterosexuality and sport.

Pat Griffin's 1992 work was critical in laying out what homophobia looks like in the athletic environ. She argues that manifestations of homophobia can be divided into six categories: silence, denial, apology, promotion of heterosexy images, attacks on lesbians, and preferences for male coaches (p.253-257). Yet her work moves beyond such descriptions to an analysis of what keeps people from fighting against homophobia: the relationship between feminism and butch lesbianism, the idea that women's sexual identity is personal, the belief that lesbians are bad role models and sexual predators, and that women's sport *can* progress without dealing with homophobic issues (p.258-261). Griffin leaves the reader with five goals that we need to focus on to dismantle homophobia in sports: institutional policy, education, visibility, solidarity, and social movement activity (p. 261-263).

Caudwell (1999) similarly addresses the butch image in sport, but investigates the experiences of female football players in the UK during the football season of 1997-1998. Her work analyzes data from 437 questionnaires, coupled with data from 14 semi-structured interviews with players. Her findings explore the stereotypes in football, but particularly the association between lesbianism and football players (p. 396). She notes how some players create a feminine image to counter such images (similar to data seen in Griffin's work), and yet Caudwell argues that too often the stereotype of lesbian and butch has often "marked all players indiscriminately" (p.401).

Keats (2016) argues in her work that "the central contention is that homophobia, an irrational fear of and negative attitude towards homosexuals, and particularly lesbophobia, fear and negativity towards lesbians, impedes all female coaching careers" (p.79). She notes that lesbians face what she calls a "double discrimination due to their gender as well as their sexual orientation" (p.80). She argues that women's integration into sport poses a threat to "the pervasive hegemony of heterosexual masculinity" (p.88). Keats shows (using Griffin's work) that the use of the lesbian label is meant as a control that "enables male, heterosexist privilege to remain in athletics" (p.82). Her work presents another valuable overview of literature on homophobia in sports.

I believe that the work of Norman (2012) is one of the most valuable pieces in this literature section. Her work is an in-depth qualitative analysis of 10 coaches in the UK, who all self-identify as lesbians. Their narratives point to how women, particularly lesbians, are often undervalued in sport. In addition, their stories tell of homophobic and sexist language usage, little governing body support, and the invisibility of women role models in sports (p. 718).

References

Acosta, R.V., & Carpenter, L.J. (1985). Status of women in athletics: Changes and causes. *Journal of Physical Education, Recreation, and Dance, 56*(8), 35-37. https://doi -org.library.smcvt.edu/10.1080/07303084.1985.10603790

Acosta, R.V., & Carpenter, L.J. (1988). Women in intercollegiate sport: A longitudinal study eleven year update, 1977-1988. Brooklyn, NY: Photocopied Report.

Acosta, R.V., & Carpenter, L.J. (2009). Are we there yet?" *Academe.* Vol. 95. No.4, (July – August), 22-24.

Allen, J.B., & Shaw, S. (2013). An interdisciplinary approach to examining the working conditions of women coaches. *International Journal Of Sports Science & Coaching, 8*(1), 1-18. https://doi-org.library.smcvt.edu/10.1260/1747-9541.8.1.1

Atkins, M., Johnson, D.M., Force, E., & Petrie, T.A. (2013). Do I still want to play? Parents' and peers' influence on girls' continuation in sport. *Journal of Sport Behavior* 36(4), 329–45.

Basford, T.E., Offermann, L.R., & Behrend, T.S. (2014). Do you see what I see? Perceptions of gender microaggressions in the workplace. *Psychology of Women Quarterly.* Vol 38, Issue 3, 340 – 349. https://doi-org.library.smcvt.edu/10.1177 /0361684313511420

Black, M.I. (2018, February 21). The boys are not all right. *New York Times,* Retrieved from http://ww.nytimes.com /2018/02/21/opinion/boys-violence-shootings-guns.html

Blank, D. (2014). *Everything your coach never told you because you're a girl: and other truths about winning.* (n.p.): SoccerPoet LLC.

Borden, S., Eder, S., Williams, J., & Harress, C. (2014, July 15). Qatari soccer empire buys a foothold in Europe. *New York Times*. Retrieved from http://www.nytimes.com/2014/07/16 /sports/worldcup/a-qatari-soccer-program-looking-to-rise -buys-a-foothold-in-europe.html

Brennan, C. (2006). *Best seat in the house: A father, a daughter, a journey through sports.* New York: Scribner.

Brooks, D. (2015, April 11). The moral bucket list. *New York Times*. Retrieved from http:// www.nytimes.com/2015/04/12 /opinion/sunday/david-brooks-the-moral-bucket-list.html

Carr E.C., & Worth A. (2001). The use of the telephone interview for research. *NT Research*. 6, 511–524. https://doi-org .library.smcvt.edu/10.1177/136140960100600107

Caudwell, J. (1990). Women's football in the UK: Theorizing gender and unpacking the butch lesbian image. *Journal of Sport and Social Issues*, 23(4), 390-402. https://doi-org .library.smcvt.edu/10.1177/0193723599234003

Caudwell, J. (2003). Sporting gender: Women's footballing bodies as sites/sights for the (re) articulation of sex, gender and desire. *Sociology of Sport Journal* 20, 371–86. https://doi-org.library.smcvt.edu/10.1123/ssj.20.4.371

Caudwell, J. (2011). Gender, feminism and football studies. *Soccer and Society* 12(3), 330–44. https://doi-org.library.smcvt.edu/10.1080/14660970.2011.568099

Chokshi, N. (2018, April 7). Do men think they're better at science than women do?...well, actually. *New York Times*. *Retrieved from* http:// www.nytimes.com/2018/04/07/science/men-women-science.html

Coffin, K. (2009). Coaching girls: a survival guide. *Coaching Quarterly*: Winter, 4-7, Retrieved from https:// www.wiaa.com/ConDocs/Con470/Coaching%20Girls.pdf

Connley, C. (2018, May 31). 41% of men say they've never heard of the #metoo movement. *CNBC*. Retrieved from http://uk.finance.yahoo.com/news/41-percent-men-apos-ve-191400381.html?guccounter=1

Cooper, M., Hunt, K., & Camille, P.O. (2007). Women in coaching: Exploring female athletes' interest in the profession. *Chronicle of Kinesiology & Physical Education in Higher Education,* 18(2), 8-19.

Cunningham, G.B., & Sagas, M. (2003). Treatment discrimination among assistant coaches of women's teams. *Research Quarterly for Exercise and Sport, 74*(4), 455-66. https://doi-org.library.smcvt.edu/10.1080/02701367.2003.10609115

Danielsen, L., Rodahl, S., Giske, R., & Heigaard, Rune. (2017). Mental toughness in elite and sub-elite female soccer players. *International Journal of Applied Sports Sciences* 29(1), 77-85. https://doi-org/10.24985/ijass.2017.29.1.77

DeLench, B. (2015). Youth sports organizations: Six ways to increase accountability, transparency. Retrieved from https:// www.momsteam.com/successful-parenting/community -oversight-of-private-youth-sports-programs-needed

Demers, G. (2007). To coach or not? *Soccer Journal.* National Soccer Coaches Association of America, 53(3): May/June, 24-30.

Derks, B., Van Laar, C., Ellemers, N., & de Groot, K. (2011). Gender-bias primes elicit queen-bee responses among senior policewomen. *Psychological Science.* Vol 22(10), 1243-1249. https://doi-org.library.smcvt .edu/10.1177/095679j7611417258

Derks, B., Van Laar, C., & Ellemers, N. (2015). The queen bee phenomenon: Why women leaders distance themselves from junior women. *The Leadership Quarterly,* 27, 456-469. https:// doi-org.library.smcvt.edu/10.1016/j.leaqua.2015.12.007

Dixon, K. (2014). How to warm the chilly climate, woman-to -woman. *Women in Higher Education.* Vol 22(10). 8-9. https:// doi-org.library.smcvt.edu/10.1002/whe.10506

Drape, J. (2018, July 14). Youth soccer participation has fallen significantly in america. *New York Times.* Retrieved from http://www.nytimes.com/2018/07/14/sports/world-cup/soccer

-youth-decline.html?hpw&rref=sports&action=click&pgtype
=Homepage&module=well-region&region=bottom-well&WT
.nav=bottom-well

Fanchini, M., Ghielmetti, R., Coutts, A. J., Schena, F., & Impellizzeri, F.M. (2015). Effect of training-session intensity distribution on session rating of perceived exertion in soccer players. *International Journal Of Sports Physiology & Performance,* 10(4), 426-430. https://doi-org.library.smcvt .edu/10.1123/ijspp.2014-0244

Fasting, K., & Pfister, G. (2000). Female and male coaches in the eyes of female elite soccer players. European Physical Education Review. 6(1), 91-110. https://doi-org.library .smcvt.edu/10.1177/1356336X000061001

Feist-Price, S. (1994). Cross-gender mentoring relationships critical issues. *The Journal of Rehabilitation.* April-June, 1994, Vol. 60 Issue 2, 13-18.

Feldblum, C.R., & Lipnic, V.A. (2016, June). Select task force on the study of harassment in the workplace. U.S. equal employment opportunity commission. Retrieved from http:// www.eeoc.gov/eeoc/task_force/harassment/report.cfm

Fielding-Lloyd, E., & Mean, L. (2011). 'I don't think I can catch it': Women, confidence, and responsibility in football coach education. *Soccer & Society* 12(3), 345–64. https://doi-org .library.smcvt.edu/10.1080.14660970.2011.568102

Foster-Simeon, E. (2013). What does it take to get our kids in the game? *Soccer Journal, 58(3),* 26–29.

Gerth H.H., & Mills, C.W. (1946) *From max weber: Essays in sociology.* New York: Oxford University Press, 77–128.

George, M. (2005). Making sense of muscle: The body experiences of collegiate women athletes. *Sociological Inquiry* 75(3), 317-345. https://doi-org.library.smcvt.edu/10.1111/j.1475-682X.2005.00125.x

Goffman, E. (1959). *Presentation of self in everyday life.* New York, NY: Anchor Books.

Greendorfer, S., & Rubinson, L. (1997). Homophobia and heterosexism in women's sport and physical education: a review. *Women in Sport & Physical Activity Journal*, 6(2), 189-210. https://doi-org.library.smcvt.edu/10.1123/wspaj.6.2.189

Griffin, P. (1992). Changing the game: Homophobia, sexism and lesbians in sport. *Quest*, 44(2), 251-265. https://doi-org.library.smcvt.edu/10.1080/00336297.1992.10484053

Hamilton, E. (1969). *Mythology: Timeless tales of gods and heroes.* New York, NY: Grand Central Publishing.

Haner, J. (2007). *Soccerhead: An accidental journey into the heart of the american game.* New York, NY: North Point Press.

Haugen, T.A., Tønnessen, E., Hisdal, J., & Seiler, S. (2014). The role and development of sprinting speed in soccer. *Journal of Sports Physiology and Performance* 9:3, 432-441. https://doi-org.library.smcvt.edu/10.1123/ijspp.2013-0121

Henson, S. (2012, Feb 15). What makes a nightmare sports parent and what makes a great one. Retrieved from http://www .thepostgame.com/blog/more-family-fun/201202/what-makes -nightmare-sports-parent

Hochschild, A. (1989). *The second shift*. New York: Avon.

Hull, N. (2010). Gender differences and coaching dynamics: Three takes. *Soccer Journal* (Nov/Dec): 28–32.

Humberd, B.K., & Rouse, E.D. (2016). Seeing you in me and me in you: Personal identification in the phases of mentoring relationships. *Academy of Management Review,* Vol. 41, No. 3, 435–455. https:// doi-org.library.smcvt.edu/10.5465/amr.2013.0203

Inglis, S., Danylchuk, K.E., & Pastore, D. (1996). Understanding retention factors in coaching and athletic management positions. *Journal of Sport Management,* 10, 237-249. Human Kinetics Publishers. Inc. https://doi-org.library. smcvt.edu/10.1123/jsm.10.3.237

Jeanes, R. (2011). 'I'm into high heels and make up but I still love football': Exploring gender identity and football participation with preadolescent girls." *Soccer & Society* 12(3), 402–20. https://doi-org.library.smcvt.edu/10.1080/14660970.2011.56 8107

Kaiser, C., & Spalding, K. 2015. Do women who succeed in male-dominated domains help other women? The moderating role of gender identification. *European Journal of Social Psychology,* 45: 599-608. https://doi-org.library .smcvt.edu/10.1002/ejsp.2113

Kamphoff, C.S., Armentrout, S.M., & Driska, A. (2010). The token female: Women's experiences as division I collegiate head coaches of men's teams. *Journal Of Intercollegiate Sport,* 3(2), 297-315. https://doi-org.library.smcvt.edu/10.1123/jis.3.2.297

Kanter, R.M. (1977). *Men and women of the Corporation.* New York: Basic books.

Kassing J. (2017). Confronting the female athlete paradox with humor and irony: A thematic analysis of SoccerGrlProbs youtube video content. *Sport and Society.* https://doi-org.library.smcvt.edu/10.1080/17430437.2017.1310202

Keathley, K., Himelein, M.J. & Srigley, G. (2013). Youth soccer participation and withdrawal: Gender similarities and differences. *Journal of Sport Behavior* 36(2), 171–88.

Keats, T. (2016). Lesbophobia as a barrier to women in coaching. *Taboo: The Journal Of Culture & Education,* 15(1), 79-92. https://doi-org.library.smcvt.edu/10.31390/taboo.15.1.08

Kilty, K. (2006). Women in coaching. *Sport Psychologist*, 20(2), 222-234. https://doi-org.library.smcvt.edu/10.1123/tsp.20.2.222

Knoppers, A. (1987). Gender and the coaching profession. *Quest,* 39(1), 9-22. https://doi.org.library.smcvt.edu/10.1080/00336297.1987.10483853

Kooistra, P. (2005). Bend it like Bourdieu: Class, gender and race in American youth soccer. Paper presented at the meeting of the American Sociological Association, Philadelphia, PA.

Krawcheck, S. (2016). *Sallie krawcheck explains why women don't help other women—and how to start.* Retrieved from http://fortune.com/2016/05/23/sallie-krawcheck-helping-women/

Lareau, A. (2011). *Unequal childhood: Class, race and family life.* Berkeley, CA: University of California Press.

Lockwood, P. (2006). 'Someone like me can be successful': Do college students need same-gender role models? *Psychology of Women Quarterly* 30: 36-46. https://doi-org.library.smcvt.edu/10.1111/j.1471-6402.2006.00260.x

Lofland, J., & Lofland, L. (1995). *Analyzing social settings: A guide to qualitative observation and analysis.* Belmont, CA: Wadsworth Press.

Lopez, S. (1997). *Woman on the ball: A guide to women's football.* London, UK: Scarlet Press.

Lopiano, D. (2016, June). *Women's sports foundation. Special issues for girls' and women' sports.* Retrieved from https://www.womenssportsfoundation.org/wp-content/uploads/2016/08/special-issues-guide.pdf

Madsen, R.M., Burton, L.J., & Clark, B.S. (2017). Gender role expectations and the prevalence of women assistant coaches, *Journal for the Study of Sports and Athl*etes in Education. https://doi.org.library.smcvt.edu/10.1080/19357397.2017.1315994

Mara, J.K., Thompson, K.G., Pumpa, K.L., & Ball, N.B. (2015). Periodization and physical and performance in elite female soccer players. *International Journal of Sports Physiology and Performance.* Jul;10(5), 664-669. https://doi.org.library .smcvt.edu/10.1123/ijspp.2014-0345

Martin, A., & Phillips, K. (2017). What "blindness" to gender differences helps women see and do: Implications for confidence, agency, and action in male-dominated environments. *Organizational Behavior and Human Decision Processes,* 14228-44. https://doi.org.library.smcvt.edu/10.1016/j.obhdp.2017.07.004

MGregor, J. (2018, April 24). "Corporate boards are still mostly white, mostly male — and getting even older." *Washington Post.* Retrieved from https://www.washingtonpost.com/news /on-leadership/wp/2018/04/24/corporate-boards-are-still-mostly -white-mostly-male-and-getting-even-older/?noredirect=on&utm _term=.4e7a624c52f2

Milyak, A. (2010). "Coaching women: Additional curriculum is needed." *Soccer Journal* (March-April), 51.

Mirsalari, S. (2016, Aug 19). *A long road ahead: Gender and the Rio 2016 Olympics news coverage.* Retrieved from http:// whomakesthenews.org/articles/a-long-road-ahead-gender- and-the-rio-2016-olympics-news-coverage

Mujika I., Santisteban J., Impellizzeri F.M., & Castagna, C. (2009). Fitness determinants of success in men's and women's football. *Journal of Sports Science.* Jan 15, 27(2), 107-14. https://doi-org.library.smcvt.edu/10.1080/02640410802428071

Musto, M., & McGann, P.J., (2016). "Strike a pose! The femininity effect in collegiate women's sport." *Sociology of Sport Journal* 33, 101-112.

Nathan, D.A. (2013). *Rooting for the Home Team*. Chicago, IL: University of Illinois Press.

NCAA.org. (n.d.). "Title IX frequently asked questions. " Retrieved from http://www.ncaa.org/about/resources/inclusion/title-ix -frequently-asked-questions

Norman, L. (2012). Gendered homophobia in sport and coaching: Understanding the everyday experiences of lesbian coaches. *International Review For The Sociology Of Sport,* 47(6), 705-723. https://doi-org.library.smcvt.edu/10.1177 /1012690211420487

Norman, L. (2013). The challenges facing women coaches and the contributions they can make to the profession. *International Journal Of Coaching Science,* 7(2), 3-23.

Parks, J.B., Russell, R.I.,Wood, P.H., Robertston, M.A., & Shewokis, P.A. (1995). The paradox of the contented working woman in intercollegiate athletics administration. *Research Quarterly for Exercise and Sport,* 66, 73-79. https://doi-org .library.smcvt.edu/10.1080/02701367.1995.10607657

Pastore, D.L. (1991). Male and female coaches of women's athletic teams: Reasons for entering and leaving the profession. *Journal Of Sport Management*, 5(2), 128-143. https://doi-org .library.smcvt.edu/10.1123/jsm.5.2.128

Polman, R., Walsh, D., Bloomfield, J., & Nesti, M. (2004). Effective conditioning of female soccer players. *Journal Sports Science.* Feb, 22(2):191-203. https://doi-org.library.smcvt.edu/10.1080/ 02640410310001641458

Rogers, K. (2016, Aug 18). Sure these women are winning Olympic medals, but are they single? Retrieved from https://www.nytimes.com/2016/08/19/sports/olympics/sexism-olympics-women.html

Roth, R., & Knapp, B. (2017). Gender negotiations of female collegiate athletes in the strength and conditioning environment. *Women in Sport and Physical Activity,* 25: 50-59. https://doi-org.library.smcvt.edu/10.1123/wspaj.2015-0049

Rowe, M. (1974). The progress of women in educational institutions: The saturn's rings phenomenon, a study of the minutiae of sexism which maintain discrimination and inhibit affirmative action results in corporations and non-profit institutions; *Graduate and Professional Education of Women,* American Association of University Women, 1974, pp. 1-9. Retrieved from http://mitmgmtfaculty.mit.edu/mrowe/research-publications/

Sabo, D., & Veliz, P. (2008). *Go out and play: Youth sports in America.* Retrieved from the Women's Sports Foundation website: https://www.womenssportsfoundation.org/research/article-and-report/participation-opportunity/go-out-and-play/

Sagas, M., Cunningham, G., & Teed, K. (2006). An examination of homologous reproduction in the representation of assistant coaches of women's teams. *Sex Roles*, 55(7-8), 503-510. https://doi-org.library.smcvt.edu/10.1007/s11199-006-9104-1

Sandberg, S. (2007). *Lean in: Women, work and the will to lead.* Knopf: New York.

Sandler, B.R. (2000). Education: The chilly classroom climate. In *Routledge International Encyclopedia of Women: Global Women's Issues and Knowledge* (Vol.1, pp. 481-482). New York, NY: Routledge.

Sandler, B.R. (2005). *The Chilly Climate.* Retrieved from https://sun.iwu.edu/~mgardner/Articles/chillyclimate.pdf.

Scavuzzo, D. (2015, February 2). Future of soccer versus football. *Goal Nation.* Retrieved from http://goalnation.com/future-soccer-vs-football/

Schlesinger, T., & Weigelt-Schlesinger, Y. (2012). 'Poor thing' or 'wow, she knows how to do it' – Gender stereotypes as barriers to women's qualification in the education of soccer coaches." *Soccer & Society.* 13(1), 56–72. https://doi-org.library.smcvt.edu/10.1080/14660970.2012.627167

Schultz, J. (2004). Discipline and push-up: Female bodies, femininity, and sexuality in popular representations of sports bras. *Sociology of Sport Journal,* 21, 185-205. https://doi-org.library.smcvt.edu/10.1123.ssj.21.2.185

Stark, R. (2017). Where are the women? *Champion Magazine.* Retrieved from http://www.ncaa.org/static/champion/where-are-the-women/

Steffen K., Pensgaard, A.M., & Bahr R. (2009). Self-reported psychological characteristics as risk factors for injuries in female youth football. *Scandinavian Journal of Medicine Science Sports.* Jun: 19(3), 442-51. https://doi-org.library.smcvt.edu/10.1111/j.1600-0838.2008.00797.x

Sue, D.W., Capodilupo, C.M., Torino, G.C., Bucceri, J.M., Holder, A.M., Nadal, K.L., & Esquilin, M. (2007). Racial microaggressions in everyday life: Implications for clinical practice. *American Psychologist.* Vol 62(4), May-Jun 2007, 271-286.

Sweney, M. (2016, Aug 15). Andy Murray slaps down John Inverdale's claim he was first with two tennis golds. *The Guardian.* Retrieved from https://www.theguardian .com/media/2016/aug/15/andy-murray-john-inverdale-olympic -tennis-bbc-williams

Synodinou, K. (1986). *The relationship between Zeus and Athena in the Iliad.* Retrieved from http://www.academia .edu/3682788/K._Synodinou_-_The_Relationship_Between _Zeus_And_Athena_In_The_Iliad

Tavernise, S. (2016, April 22). US suicide rates surge to 30 year high. *New York Times.* Retrieved from https://www.nytimes .com/2016/04/22/health/us-suicide-rate-surges-to-a-30-year- high.html

Thorne, B. (1993). *Gender play: Girls and boys in school.* New Brunswick, N.J: Rutgers University Press.

U.S. sending record number of women to Rio games. (2016, July 24). Retrieved from http://www.nbcolympics.com/news/us -sending-record-number-women-rio-games

Vescovi J.D., & VanHeest, J.L. (2010). Effects of an anterior cruciate ligament injury prevention program on performance in adolescent female soccer players. *Scandinavian Journal*

Medicine Science Sports. Jun; 20(3), 394-402. https://doi -org.library.smcvt.edu/10.111/j.1600-0838.2009.00963.x

Vescovi, J.D., & Favero, T. (2014). Motion characteristics of women's college soccer matches: Female athletes in motion (FAiM) study. *International Journal of Sports Physiology and Performance,* 9, 405-414. https://doi-org.library.smcvt .edu/10.1123/IJSPP.2013-0526

Vincent, A., & Seymour, J. (1995). Profile of women mentors: A national survey. *Advanced Management Journal* 60(2) 4-10.

Wahl, G. (2017, April 5). U.S. Women, U.S. Soccer agree to new CBA, end labor dispute. Retrieved from https://www.si.com/ planet-futbol/2017/04/05/uswnt-us-soccer-women-cba-labor-talks-agreement

Way, N. (2016, January 12). Why we should celebrate all mentors, male and female. *The Chronicle of Evidence-Based Mentoring.* Retrieved from https://chronicle.umbmentoring. org/niobe-way-professor-of-applied-developmental-psychol ogy-at-nyu-and-author-of-deep-secrets/

Webber, A.M. (1998, January 31). *Is your job calling: Extended interview.* Retrieved from https://www.fastcompany. com/33545/your-job-your-calling-extended-interview

Welch, S., & Sigelman, L. (2007). Who's calling the shots? Women coaches in division I women's sports. *Social Science Quarterly*, 88, 1415-1434. Retrieved from http://www.jstor .org/stable/42956250

Welford, Jo. (2011). Tokenism, ties and talking too quietly: Women's experiences in non-playing football roles. *Soccer and Society* 12(3), 365–81.

West, C., & Zimmerman, D. (1987). Doing gender. *Gender and Society, 1*(2), 125-151. Retrieved from http://www.jstor.org/stable/189945.

Wife of bears lineman wins a bronze medal. (2016, August 7). Retrieved from https://twitter.com/chicagotribune/status/762401317050605568?lang=en

Wilson, J. (2007). Homer and the will of Zeus. *College Literature*, 34(2), 150-173. Retrieved from http://www.jstor.org/stable/25115425